The God Nudge

Learning to flow in the supernatural.

Mike D. Robertson

Cover photos by Andrew Sea James Photography, Las Vegas, NV
Front cover design by Jered Miller, Visalia, California
Dust cover layout and interior formatting by Anita Louise Lessel, Visalia, California

ISBN 978-1-4675-3478-9

Published by MDR Quest, Inc.

Dedication

To the most gracious people Karen and I have ever met:

Visalia First Assembly of God

Every Pastor should have a Church like this,
at least once, in their ministry career.

Contents

Introduction. 9

Chapter 1 Welcome To The Nudge. 17
Chapter 2 It's Not As Hard As You Think. 25
Chapter 3 Escaping Ordinary. 45
Chapter 4 Learning to Discern. 59
Chapter 5 Overcoming God Nudge Obstacles. 75
Chapter 6 Risk-Takers. 99
Chapter 7 Nudges and Money. 115
Chapter 8 The Thrill of Being Spirit-Filled. 127

Using The God Nudge in Classes and Groups. 147

About the Author. 151

Resources

Introduction

Seven Magical Words

As you think, so shall you be!

Have you ever wondered why some people are successful in life? It seems like everything they touch turns to gold. On the other hand, have you ever wondered why some people just can't seem to get it together? Everything they touch just seems to go kaput or fizzles out.

It has become clearer to me that people who are happy and fully functioning are able to attract what they want in life; and that the opposite is true as well … if a person is unhappy and is laden with problems, they just can't seem to attract the good out of life.

I believe that the number one reason people cannot get what they want in life is because they are spending too much energy on what they do NOT want! If I asked you: "Do you want depression?" You would say, "No!" But why do we constantly get out of bed thinking: "I'm not feeling so hot today. Guess I'll be depressed." If I asked you if you wanted arthritis, you would say, "No way!" But why is it just a pain can shoot through our body and we begin to focus on arthritis, the thing we do not want. It's hard to attract the good things when you are always dwelling on the negative. As you think, so shall you be.

Picture yourself driving down a freeway and you get an ugly thought. The more you dwell on it, the more you are thinking about it. Now, picture the same scenario, but you are thinking about a happy thought … a God thought. You and I have to do this multiple times every day of our lives. You have to decide: Do I take the exit ramp to Negative Town, or do I take the ramp that leads me to Happyville? Whichever place you choose, those types of people are going to greet you with their thoughts as well.

So the next question is: How can I think better thoughts? Let me show you how to tap into God thoughts. God thoughts are where we get God Nudges.

LIVING OUTSIDE OF FORM

Romans 12:2 tells us, "Be not conformed but be transformed by the renewing of your mind." Split the word "conformed" and what is the middle word: *form*. Split the word "transformation" and you get the word *form* again. This is the basis for this book. God has a life for us outside of FORM!

Be not conformed... "Con" appears as a prefix to words like convict, confined, constrict or conceal. In the Greek, "con" is *suschematizo*, which means: to conform one's self (i.e. one's mind and character) to another's pattern; to fashion one's self according to another's pattern. Paul is saying that we are not to be conformed, constrained or constricted to our natural physical form – *but be transformed ...* "Trans" is a prefix to words like translate, transfer or transcend. Webster defines the prefix "trans" as: across, on the other side of, beyond. Basically, we must find a life outside of our physical form. We can do that. Followers of Christ are the best candidates.

We are so accustomed to only thinking of ourselves as a physical being, not a spiritual one. We live in a culture that reinforces this belief, and so we treat ourselves as a "form" whose contents are irrelevant. To be "transformed" is the ability to rise above "form" – the physical you – that would be your bones, skin, toenails, and blood vessels. It is interesting to note that 95% of what is contained in our physical form can also be found in a pig!

When you live exclusively by form, you live in a world of limitations. You can only lift so much, run so fast, work so hard.

However, if you would consider for a moment that there is a part of you without physical boundaries, there is no limit to your ability to think. You can imagine yourself doing something you haven't done before. You can imagine a great relationship with your spouse. Whenever you imagine these possibilities in your mind, you are experiencing life in the dimension that transcends your limited physical form.[1]

I heard a story of a man who was frantically searching for his lost keys outside under a streetlight. A lady walked by, noticed his frantic state and asked him what he was looking for. "I dropped my keys," the man stated. The lady said she would help him look for them. After thirty minutes of fruitless searching, the lady asked, "Where did you drop them?" "I dropped them inside the house" the man replied. Confused, the woman then asked, "But why are you looking outside of your house for your keys if you dropped them inside?" "Because the light is better out here," he replied. Now, that's a silly story, but this is precisely what we do every time we look outside ourselves for a solution.

It seems much easier for us to define ourselves by our form rather than defining ourselves by the inner qualities we cannot see, taste or touch. It's easier because that is how everyone else is doing it and we have a great need to fit in with the crowd. If you suggest to a young person that they should separate from the crowd, they would most likely tell you they don't want to be weird or an oddball.

Sadly, we are simply unwilling to take the criticism that goes with thinking independently.

[1]Wayne W. Dyer (2001), *You'll See It When You Believe It,* New York, NY, HarperCollins

Everyone Can Participate In The God Nudge

A friend of mine follows Christ. I told him I was writing a book entitled: The God Nudge. He got a puzzled look on his face, so I began to explain to him that it is about how we flow in the supernatural. That's when I really lost him. He said he had never flowed in the supernatural. To my astonishment I said, "You can. Everyone can flow in the God Nudge if you will get outside your five senses and tap into the jet stream of God."

Our mind is a powerful tool. It is capable of transcending form. Every one of us has a sixth sense – and when we can learn to tap into that sixth sense, the sky is the limit as to what we can dream, what we can accomplish, and what we can do for God.

The God Nudge was written to teach you to tap into a life that transcends your five senses – to empower the spiritual being that is within each of us, and to live the life we, as followers of Christ, were called to live.

I, like many, have read the Bible numerous times. I have always thought: "It would be nice to be used of God like the Old Testament prophets and Jesus." It would be very easy to excuse myself and say, "Signs and wonders only follow the super saints." I actually used to think that.

> *"You must live your life in a way that you show up in someone else's testimony."*
> *– Jim Rohn*

Then I changed my thinking. I began asking God to use me in signs and wonders. The Bible says, "These signs will follow those who believe..." (Mark 16:17). For years now I have focused on and expected God to show me the supernatural every day. Guess what? It has happened. Every church service, I see signs and wonders because I am focused on what I what to happen, rather than on the things I don't want to happen.

Throughout these chapters, you will discover people from the Bible who tapped into their sixth sense. The things they accomplished through their God Nudges are the very things we are still talking about today. Jim Rohn put it best: "You must live your life in a way that you show up in someone else's testimony." The God Nudge insures that. Before you exit this planet, you need to develop some stories that people will be talking about after your lifetime. Who knows ... what you thought you were not able to accomplish in your lifetime, may actually be accomplished in your lifeline!

Mike D. Robertson

A God Nudge – Defined

Discernment, an insight, foreknowledge
(n.) A spiritual premonition, feeling or sense; an illumination
(v.) A spiritual prod or push

Chapter 1

Welcome To The Nudge

Several years ago, my wife, Karen, and I were talking one Saturday night about the will of God for our lives and what the future held for us. We'd both been serving the Lord for quite a few years and always desired to be where God wanted us to be. Yet, I had a stirring in my soul that a change was coming. We were trying to process what I felt God was saying to me. The direction wasn't clear, so we decided to continue to pray. We trusted God to give us a clear word from heaven.

We were living in Oceanside, California, just north of San Diego where we were the founding pastors of a wonderful church. We loved the city, we loved the people, and we loved Southern California—but there was a tugging in our hearts to make a change. We knew this was going to be a very important decision, and we didn't want to make a mistake.

The next day, as I was getting ready to preach on a beautiful Sunday morning, I was alerted by one of the leaders in my church that a man named Harald Bredesen had stepped into our service. He was one of the most unique people on earth. He was a former Lutheran pastor who was baptized in the Holy Spirit. In fact, some have said it was Bredesen who gave the name "charismatic" to the Spirit-filled movement.

That morning, Karen led us in a wonderful time of worship. We experienced the presence and the blessing of the Lord. I then asked Harald, "Would you like to say anything to the people here at Family Fellowship?"

Harald was well into his 80s, and he walked slowly to the front of the church. He had been deeply moved during the worship time. As he spoke to us, he began to cry. He said he had never felt the presence of God as he had in our worship service that day. He announced that the Lord had a message for us: He wanted us to take our worship experience beyond the walls of our church. We needed to share this kind of worship with others—not only nationwide, but also worldwide.

My heart sensed, "That's it!" Harald's words were the confirmation Karen and I were looking for. We'd been trying to determine if it was God's will for us to leave the church in Oceanside and take a position at Southwestern University, an Assemblies of God college near Dallas, Texas. That one God Nudge—the word from Harald Bredesen—confirmed in my spirit what the Lord had been speaking to me for a long time. But Harald's message wasn't just for me. Karen had been very hesitant about leaving our church. Now she was convinced God had given us clear, unmistakable direction.

After preparing for the transition, Karen and I moved to our new assignment, which turned out to be one of the most strategic decisions we had ever made. I became the Vice President of Advancement at the university, and Karen became a Pastor over the chapel worship. Thousands of young people learned from her as she led and taught them how to worship. Today, people all over the world are sharing what Karen planted in their hearts. It was the fulfillment of God's Word through Harald Bredesen. Our sense of God's leading, however, hadn't been clear until we experienced a God Nudge.

God nudges us in many different ways.

God Nudges us in many different ways. His Spirit may speak to us through a passage of Scripture. As we read, the Holy Spirit "illumines" the truth to give us encouragement, direction, or correction. A nudge may come from the advice of a leader or a mature Christian friend. God often uses circumstances. He may put up a roadblock to steer our path, or He may open a door for us. God leads some people in visions and dreams. In this book, I want to focus on one particular type of God Nudge: the whisper of the Spirit. In several passages in the Bible, the writers describe the Spirit's desire and ability to lead us. In fact, Paul says that the Spirit's leading is like the intimate relationship of a parent and child. Just as a loving, attentive parent wants to guide his or her child in life's decisions, our Heavenly Father wants to direct us, too. Paul wrote:

> "For those who are led by the Spirit of God are the children of God." (Romans 8:14)

Some people attend church regularly, but they're just going through the motions. They sing the songs and put some money in the offering basket, but as soon as they walk out the door, they forget about God for the rest of the week. Others long to connect with God, but they assume their flaws and faults disqualify them from having a real, rich, meaningful relationship with God. The good news of the gospel is that the sovereign, Almighty God of the universe has paid the ultimate price for you and me so that we can truly know Him. As a loving Father, He wants a give-and-take relationship. The fact that God wants to communicate with His children shouldn't come as a surprise. In the opening lines of John's Gospel, he makes the dramatic statement:

> "In the beginning was the Word, and the Word was with God, and the Word was God." (John 1:1)

John says that Jesus Christ is "the Word." It's His very nature to communicate with those He loves—including every person in the world.

As we'll see in this book, God delights in nudging His children, but we don't play a passive role. We have to cultivate a sensitive heart to respond to Him. And like every form of interpersonal communication, we sometimes misunderstand. When we interpret a God Nudge incorrectly it's not the end of the world and it doesn't mean we're inferior Christians. We just need to learn to discern His voice.

We need to remember, though, that we're connecting to the Creator of the universe. God is "as close as our breath," but He's "far above all." He stoops to connect with us the way a loving parent bends to show love to a child. One of the greatest privileges in life is to have a rich, real relationship with the God of all. The disciples were amazed that Jesus walked among them and related to them. Today, His Spirit lives within us and wants to relate to us every minute of every day.

When I was growing up in Littlefield, Texas—which also happens to be the hometown of country singer, Waylon Jennings—I had a paper route. As a young man barely in junior high school, I was assigned a street called Mocking Bird Lane. Before dawn each day, I threw papers on porches and in yards. For some reason the city hadn't installed adequate streetlights on this street, so I had to ride my bike in the dark. I quickly learned that the owner of the newspaper wasn't concerned about my fears. He was concerned only that his paying customers got their newspapers. Every morning, I had to fight through my fears to complete my route on Mocking Bird Lane.

Over the years, I've thought a lot about the lesson I learned from my first job. God wants to deliver important messages—He wants to answer people's prayers. But His greatest challenge is finding people who will overcome their fears, listen to Him, and let Him use them to transform lives.

> "When the Pharisee, Simon, who had invited Him saw this, he said to himself, 'If this man were a prophet, He would know who is touching Him and what kind of woman she is—that she is a sinner.' Jesus answered him, 'Simon, I have something to tell you.' "
> (Luke 7:39-40)

It's amazing to me how Jesus was able to read Simon's thoughts, and I've often thought that it would be very cool if we could do that. The Bible says I CAN do that!

> "... whatever you ask the Father in My name He will give you." (John 16:23)

I don't know that it literally means that we would audibly hear what someone else was thinking, but I do believe that God can give us the ability to perceive another's thoughts.

Another amazing example from the Bible is the story of the time that Jesus went to the house of Mary and Martha, and Mary sat at Jesus' feet while Martha busied herself doing meaningless household chores. Here is the Son of God sitting in her house, and Martha is worried about cleaning the kitchen! Jesus said that Mary had chosen a better thing.

I find myself a lot like Mary. I am a sinner who is incredibly interested in the supernatural side of life. What prompted Mary to anoint Jesus' feet? I think it was a God Nudge so strong that she was able to break through the good-'ol-boys club and just sit at the feet of Jesus like the other disciples were doing. Jesus applauded her faith and said to her, "... Go in peace, your faith has saved you." (Luke 7:50)

It is my belief that thousands of God's desires are going unfulfilled daily on the earth. Too many people are receiving God Nudges, but are simply ignoring them. Let's not wait until we get to heaven before we realize what could have, and what should have, been done.

Are you listening to God's whispers? Are you willing to learn to respond to God's Nudges? When He gives you a nudge, will you respond in faith and obedience? That's the adventure of the Christian life. The historian of the Chronicles wrote:

> "For the eyes of the Lord range throughout the earth to strengthen those whose hearts are fully committed to Him." (2 Chronicles 16:9)

He's still looking for people like that today. I'm in. Are you?

As you make your way through the contents of this book, make it your daily prayer to be used in a God Nudge. And make it your daily belief that God will do for you what He has done for thousands of others: He has made them His ambassadors who serve as a pipeline, a transportation service for heaven to bring about positive change (the expansion of God's Kingdom) on the earth.

At the end of each chapter you'll find some questions to help you think and pray about what you've read. Take your time in answering them. The goal isn't to "fill in the blanks," but to trust God to help you apply the principles in the chapters. The questions are also designed to promote discussion in classes and groups. I trust God will use these questions to stimulate your faith, deepen your understanding of His leading, and prompt you to be obedient when He nudges you.

Think about it...

1. How have you seen God use His Word, the advice of mature Christians, circumstances, and the whisper of the Spirit to communicate a message and change the direction of people's lives?

2. Which of these has God used most often in your life? How do you normally respond?

3. Do you expect God to nudge you? Why or why not?

4. What do you hope to get out of this book?

Chapter 2

It's Not As Hard As You Think

What's a God Nudge? It's when God puts a feeling in your heart and a thought in your head that just won't go away. He may prompt you to show kindness to a stranger, speak a word of hope to a friend, or give something you value to someone—maybe someone you don't even know. God Nudges are often His leading to take action in an extraordinary way. They're often challenging, so they may remind us to trust God instead of our own wisdom and strength. The whispers of the Spirit can come at any time. In fact, they often come when we least expect them.

Many years ago, Karen and I were pastoring a church in Texas. One day while I was praying, the Lord nudged me, telling me that I needed to go to San Diego. The thought was crystal clear, but it made no sense at all. I was too busy to go to San Diego, so I explained to the Lord that I simply couldn't go. After all, I'd just been on a long trip. I was tired, and I had a lot of work to catch up on. My answer was completely reasonable, but God wasn't finished with me. He nudged me again: "I need you in San Diego next week."

This time, I began to negotiate with the Lord, "Lord, if this is really You, I need someone to give me a free airline ticket. That's how I'll know."

The next morning, I went to a Men's Breakfast at the church. After the meeting had concluded, a local businessman came up to me and announced, "Hey Pastor, do you know anybody who needs an airline ticket?"

I didn't connect the dots at first. I answered, "No, not really."

He continued, "My wife and I have a ticket for a flight anywhere in the United States. If somebody doesn't use it by next Friday, it's going to expire. I want to give it away."

Suddenly, a light went on in my brain: "Does the airline fly to San Diego?"

He answered, "Oh, yeah."

I responded, "I'll take it."

Sometimes God's biggest challenge is getting through my thick skull. I still didn't know why God wanted me to go to San Diego, so I called my friend, Ken Squires, who lived in the city. I hesitantly told him, "The Lord told me to come over there to help you. Do you need any help?"

He enthusiastically replied, "Mike, I'm glad you called. We're taking young people into Mexico, and I really do need some help. When can you come?"

A few days later I was in San Diego helping Ken and his team prepare young people for ministry in Mexico. It was a wonderful time, but it was even more special because God had not only prompted me to go, He also provided the resources. Over the years that have ensued, God has used Ken's ministry, called Sun City, to lead many people to Christ. Thousands of American teenagers have traveled to Mexico during the summer months to take food and medical supplies to less fortunate people. In addition, the ministry has planted over a dozen churches. I'd always been amazed at Ken's ministry, and I am so glad that I had the great privilege of being part of it.

God Nudges are important, but it's easy to discount them. Usually, they aren't about major changes of direction in our careers. Instead, God gives us the idea to stop to talk to a lonely person or share with someone in need. The person may be our spouse, child, parent, or they may be a total stranger. We need discernment though, to know whether the feeling is from God or the gastronomic result of last night's pizza!

Wrong Assumptions

Bruce Wilkinson is one of my favorite authors. He wrote the New York Times #1 Bestseller, *The Prayer of Jabez.* I've bought hundreds of these books and passed them out. He wrote another book entitled, *You Were Born For This: Seven Keys To A Life of Predictable Miracles.* While I was reading this book, God Nudges became much clearer for me. In the book, Bruce asks a simple but insightful question, "What do you think is going on in heaven right now?"

Most Christians have never thought deeply about the current realities in heaven. I've been a student of the Bible for many years. In my reading, I've seen many instances throughout the Scriptures when God unzips the fabric of heaven and gives us a glimpse of what's going on. It's amazing! Years ago, I had a near-death experience, so I had a brief taste of eternity. Since that time, I've had a hunger for heaven, and I've imagined what's happening just outside our dimensions of time and space. Many of us, though, have wrong assumptions about heaven and our interaction with the supernatural world. Let's examine a few.

• Wrong Assumption #1:
God can get our attention if and when He needs to.

Yes, He certainly can get our attention. The Scriptures are full of examples of God breaking into our world to communicate with us. He used a burning bush, plagues, a pillar of cloud, fire from heaven, storms, whirlwinds, prophets, and many other methods. However, God doesn't normally use dramatic ways to communicate with His people. He's looking for people whose hearts are tender and receptive. He wants a relationship with people who are sensitive to His gentle whisper. We need to be open to God and say, "God, I'm available. Speak to me. Send me on a miracle mission." Is this the attitude of your heart?

Sadly, some people have an attitude that says, "God knows my address. He's a big God. He knows where to find me if He needs me to do something. Until then, I'm doing my own thing." There's more than a little arrogance wrapped up in this statement. We need to come in humility and say, "Lord, I'm yours. I sure would like to do something for You, God. Will you lead me?" A humble, open heart makes all the difference.

The Bible tells us that Isaiah was in church one day, and he was grieving over the death of his cousin, King Uzziah. While he was praying, he got caught up in a vision. He saw a board meeting going on in heaven. God and His angels were looking for someone to go preach the gospel. Isaiah responded: "Here am I, send me" (Isaiah 6:8).

We need to come in humility and say, "Lord, I'm yours."

One day while I was preaching at our church in Visalia, California, I posed the question to our congregation that Bruce Wilkinson asked in his book: "What do you think is going on in heaven right now?" I asked everyone in the audience to use their cell phones and text their answer to phone numbers that we had set up.

That day, hundreds of people in the worship service text messaged us their answers, but I do not believe any one of them got the answer correct. Not one. They gave the standard answers: worshiping around the throne of God, getting to visit with loved ones, there's no more crying and no more pain. But no one hit the nail on the head.

I personally believe a series of staff meetings are going on in heaven right now. Yes, all the things mentioned by people in our worship service are happening, but heaven is also having staff meetings. God and the angels are discussing the prayers and petitions of people on earth and are working to see how they are going to answer literally millions of prayers.

People all over the world are praying. They're asking God to bless them and help them with a difficult situation. Heaven then has to process those prayers and find someone on earth they can use to deliver the answer to the prayer. The angels sometimes appear to do God's work, but every time one of them shows up, people freak out! Far more often, God uses people like you and I.

Does this sound strange to you? It shouldn't. The Bible says we're God's children who have been entrusted with the family business of taking His grace to every person on the planet (Matthew 28:18-20). We are joint heirs with Christ (Romans 8:17), and ambassadors for Him (2 Corinthians 5:20). We have a new identity and a new purpose. Peter described it this way:

> "But you are a chosen people, a royal priesthood, a holy nation, God's special possession, that you may declare the praises of Him who called you out of darkness into His wonderful light." (1 Peter 2:9)

God has entrusted the greatest enterprise in the world to us, but He hasn't left us alone. He is with us. He promises to guide us, empower us, and use us to change lives.

God is looking for people who will be partners with Him. He wants to deliver a message of faith, hope, and love, and He has chosen us to be His delivery agents. He needs humble, responsive believers who will be the answer to a person's prayer.

God wants to use every single one of us to help answer those prayers. Are you open to a God Nudge?

• Wrong Assumption #2:
We don't have any responsibility when God is performing miracles.

Yes, we do. God's agenda is our responsibility. God sometimes works apart from people to accomplish His purposes, but far more often, He chooses to use us in His grand plan to redeem the world and build His kingdom. He doesn't need us, but He graciously let's us participate in His work in people's lives. The disciples saw Jesus do incredible miracles, but He told them,

> "Very truly I tell you, whoever believes in Me will do the works I have been doing, and they will do even greater things than these, because I am going to the Father." (John 14:12)

Being God's partner in answering prayer takes faith, dedication, and tenacity. Miracles seldom happen when we are complacent.

• Wrong Assumption #3:
Doing the work of God is out of our reach.

Certainly, we're deeply flawed. In fact, the more we grow in our relationship with Christ, the more we become aware of the darkness in our hearts. But as we grow, we also realize the incredible privilege of God using broken people like us. It's one of the marks of His great grace! When you feel like a loser, don't despair. Remember that God's kingdom is upside down. The arrogant and self-righteous disqualify themselves, but those who admit they're flawed are right where God wants them to be: humble, receptive, and open. The Bible tells us that God even used a donkey to deliver a message to a man that ignored a God Nudge. If God can use a donkey, He can use you and I! The responsibility to change the lives of others isn't ours; it's God's. We're just the delivery agents. We're successful when we're obedient to God's prompting to step into a person's life. From that point, it's between God and that person.

• Wrong Assumption #4:
We must make ourselves more worthy.

Let me give you a newsflash: You'll never be worthy enough! Too many times, we wait or we hesitate because we think we have to be squeaky clean before we can become a vessel of God. It will never happen. Paul wrote the Corinthians,

> "But we have this treasure in jars of clay to show that this all-surpassing power is from God and not from us." (2 Corinthians 4.7)

A sensitive spirit is essential, but it can have a dark side. If we let them, guilt, shame, and self-doubt will sidetrack us. Every time I preach, I think of something that I shouldn't have done or a dumb thing I said during the previous week. There's always something! At those moments, I can beat myself up for being such a jerk, or I can thank God for His wonderful forgiveness. If He was willing to restore Peter for denying Him three times, I can be sure He will forgive me, too.

Thoughts of self-condemnation are a trick of the enemy to make you think you're disqualified. Our qualifications aren't based on our perfection, but only on God's grace. He's the one who qualifies us. Paul wrote the Colossians that we give thanks –

> "...to the Father, who has qualified you to share in

the inheritance of His holy people in the kingdom of light. For He has rescued us from the dominion of darkness and brought us into the kingdom of the Son He loves, in whom we have redemption, the forgiveness of sins." (Colossians 1:12-14)

So . . . go ahead and respond to that God Nudge. You're qualified by God's grace. He loves you, forgives you, accepts you, and calls you His partner.

• WRONG ASSUMPTION #5:
The spiritual dimension is just too complicated and strange.

In the account of the patriarchs in Genesis, we find that when Jacob was praying, angels were going up and down from heaven to the earth. These angels were right next to him, but he didn't realize it because he couldn't step into that dimension. Jacob isn't alone. You and I are living next to a spiritual dimension—we can call it "the fourth dimension"—that's outside the physical world. The two worlds are very different, but they intersect. In fact, some Bible scholars and pastors teach that heaven is another dimension all around us. It's not "up there" at all. If we listen, if we sense a God Nudge, we'll capture a whisper from heaven. In his book, *The Fourth Dimension*, Dr. David Yongghi Cho explains:

> In the universe there are three types of spirits—the Holy Spirit of God, the spirit of the devil, and the human spirit. When you study geometry, you put up two points, one here, and one there, and if you draw a line between the two you call it one dimension. It is just one line between two points, one dimension. But if you add line upon line by the hundreds of thousands, then one dimension naturally creates

> a second dimension, a plane. And if you stack up planes one upon another then it becomes cubic; this is called the third dimension. The material world and the whole earth belong to the third dimension. This first dimension, a line, is contained in, and therefore controlled by, the second dimension, a plane; and the second dimension is included in, and therefore controlled by, the third dimension, the cube. Who then creates, contains, and controls the third dimension, the cubical world? You have the answer when you open the Bible and read in Genesis 1:2: "And the earth was without form, and void; and darkness was upon the face of the deep. And the Spirit of God moved upon the face of the waters." But if you look into the original language of that scripture, it carries the meaning that the Spirit of the Lord was incubating over the waters, brooding over the waters. This chaotic world belonged to the third dimension, but the Holy Spirit, who is pictured here incubating on the third dimension, belongs to the fourth dimension. So the spiritual kingdom of faith belongs to the fourth dimension.[2]

Yes, the spiritual dimension is different than the one we see, hear, touch, taste, and smell, but it's very real. When we understand we continually live in the seen and the unseen worlds, we will be open to God's intervention in our minds and hearts.

---

[2]Dr. David Yonggi Cho (1979) *The Fourth Dimension Volume One*, Alachua Florida, Bridge-Logos

Commit To Be Used

In order to become a delivery agent, you've got to make some commitments.

• **First**, *make a commitment to act when you receive a God Nudge.*

Wake up in the morning and renew your pledge: "God, I'm ready to act if You nudge me to talk to someone today, or if You tell me to give someone some money, or if You need me to be a miracle. I'm available." Make this statement part of your daily prayers, and remind yourself of it all day. Pray the prayer of Isaiah: "Here am I, Lord, send me. I'm a delivery agent for You."

• **Second**, *decide in advance how to deal with distractions.*

Have you ever been sidetracked? I sure have. Today, there are more devices and distractions than ever before. When we want to connect with God, we need to get away, find a quiet place, and turn off our social media. I'm a big fan of praying as we go through the day. I want to depend on God in the middle of a conversation or situation, but sometimes, I need to be alone and quiet.

When God tells you to do something, you've got to resolve in your heart, "I'm going to do this..."

For a mom, it might be hard to concentrate on praying with all the responsibilities of her children and their schedules throughout the day. Guys, you can't pray too easily if you've got the sports section of the paper open next to you. You've got to find a time and place where you're not distracted.

When God tells you to do something, you've got to resolve in your heart, "I'm going to do this. I'm not going to be distracted. God told me to go do this, and nobody can talk me out of it." We need hearts of courageous, tenacious faith.

• **Third**, *step out in faith even if you don't have all the facts.*

Some people are waiting for all the facts. They believe information brings them security, and they won't take a step until they've answered every question. These people become spiritually paralyzed. No matter how much God speaks to them, it's not enough to overcome their fears. Even after the tenth nudge, they pray, "Can you give me a little bit more, Lord? I need to know exactly what I'm supposed to do." I promise you, He's not like that. He doesn't give us the whole load of information all at once. He gives us enough, but not too much. We have to rely on His goodness and greatness instead of our ability to check off every box on our list of questions.

Let me give you a practical example. Imagine that yesterday I left an envelope of important papers at a restaurant on Bonnie Brea Street in Los Angeles, and I ask you to pick it up for me. A person that's ready to step out in faith would say, "Okay, I'll go." She doesn't wait to volunteer until she has all the answers. She trusts that the answers and resources will come as she takes steps forward. However, some people would hesitate. They would have a million questions, and for each one that's answered, ten more would appear. First, they want specific directions: "Where's Bonnie Brea Street? Is it one-way? What's the best route to get there? Will traffic be bad? I don't know if I have enough gas. What if my car breaks down? What if the envelope is gone? What does it look like?"

Questions aren't evil, but they can become a subtle way of avoiding obedience. When you get a God Nudge, ask a few questions to clarify your direction. But even if no answers come, take a step of faith and respond to God's prompting. He will give you direction as you take each step forward.

A God Nudge Collision

When you've decided to be a delivery agent for God and an answer to people's prayers, be prepared for a God Nudge collision. What's that? Quite often, it's a collision of values and heart. God often asks us to reach out to communicate love to people we don't know—and sometimes, to people we don't even like. Paul described the extent of God's amazing love:

> "God demonstrates His own love for us in this:
> While we were still sinners, Christ died for us."
> (Romans 5:8)

Isn't that good news! While you were sinning, Christ was dying for you and saying, "If you will just accept Me, your heart, your identity, your motivations, and your destiny will turn around."

As we experience God's grace, He sends us on a mission to be His voice, hands, and feet. But we don't go empty handed (or empty hearted). We love others out of the deep well of God's deep love for us (1 John 4:10-11), we forgive those who have hurt us because we've experienced Christ's forgiveness of our sins (Ephesians 4:31-32), and we accept people—even those who annoy us—because we're the glad recipients of God's complete acceptance (Romans 15:7). God Nudges often force us to look deeper into the grace of God, to experience more love, forgiveness, and acceptance than ever, so we can deliver the real thing to others. Nothing phony, nothing faked. When we realize we fall short and we don't love the people God is nudging us toward, we need to go back to the source. John described a scene in the life of Jesus that shows the supernatural source of the strength to love others. At a weeklong feast, each day's ceremonial washings and sacrifices grew in a crescendo of importance. The last day was at a fever pitch! John paints this picture:

> "On the last and greatest day of the festival, Jesus stood and said in a loud voice, 'Let anyone who is thirsty come to Me and drink. Whoever believes in Me, as Scripture has said, rivers of living water will flow from within them.' By this He meant the Spirit." (John 7:37-39)

Do you feel inadequate to respond to a God Nudge? Go back to the source of your identity as a child of God. Do you feel weak? Trust in Jesus' strength. Are you thirsty for a real relationship with God so you sense His nudges and presence? Drink deeply from Jesus, the fountain of living water.

Walking with Jesus necessarily implies a conflict of preferences. We call Him "Lord," which means Master. Is He the Master of your life? We show the content of our hearts by our willingness to obey His nudges. Sometimes, they're a lot of fun, but occasionally, answering God's call is the most threatening thing we can imagine. We may prefer safety, but a life of faith takes us where Jesus walked—to love even those who despise us, to give until it hurts, and show kindness when we'd rather criticize. Each God Nudge is a potential collision of values and preferences, but those who call Jesus "Lord" and "Master" are willing to say "No" to selfish desires so they can be His hands, feet, and voice.

We may prefer saftey, but a life of faith takes us where Jesus walked...

I was born-again when I was 19 years old at a little country church. A lady who attended the church was, to put it bluntly, nuts. I'm sure there's a psychiatric diagnosis for her condition, but the people in the church just called her "crazy." She had a look in her eye that told us the wiring in her brain was out of whack, and her communication loudly proclaimed that she was mentally unbalanced. After every phrase the preacher said, she shouted, "Amen!" It lasted the whole service . . . every Sunday . . . all year every year. In those days, preachers didn't pattern their sermons after 30-minute television programs. They often spoke for 90 minutes. During that time, this lady said "Amen!" hundreds of times. Literally. I'm not kidding. It was extremely annoying.

I was just a young man, and you can imagine how the young people made fun of her. One day, the Lord nudged me: "I want you to go tell that lady that her daughter will meet her in heaven."

I was stunned. I replied, "What, Lord? You've got to be kidding. Not her, not now, not ever. I don't even like her, Lord. She's weird, and besides, she wears that horrible perfume. Can't you find somebody else?"

I resisted the nudges for a long time, but God kept telling me, "Go tell her."

Finally, I couldn't deny that it was God speaking to me. After a service, I found the lady in the front of the church, and I stammered, "Mrs. Williams, I think … the Lord … the Lord told me to tell you that your daughter will meet you in heaven."

She went ballistic! At first, I didn't know if she was going to kill me or kiss me. Then she explained that she had been praying for her daughter for many years. She was so happy to have a word from God about her dear daughter. It meant the world to her. Suddenly, a woman who had been an object of scorn and a target of jokes, became a real, flesh-and-blood human being with deep desires, hurts, and hopes. The God Nudge meant a lot to her . . . and it changed me, too.

Mrs. Williams didn't stop being annoying to me. In fact, every Sunday she asked me, "Mike, is today the day my daughter is getting saved? Did God give you a word about that?"

And every Sunday, I reminded her, "Mrs. Williams, the Lord said she'll meet you in heaven, but that doesn't mean she's going to get saved in your lifetime. But don't worry. God's promise is true." At first, I didn't want to respond to the God Nudge, but I'm glad I finally did.

Our walks with God aren't primarily about our comfort and excitement. God's vision is for the whole world, and He uses every available means to accomplish His purpose of redemption—including asking His children to step out in faith to do things we'd rather not do. Jesus didn't want to go to the cross, but He went. If He was willing to sacrifice His life, shouldn't we be willing to sacrifice a moment of comfort and convenience? It's not about us; it's about God and His kingdom. It's not about our preferences; it's about God's passion to reach every person on earth and transform lives with His power and grace. You and I are simply His delivery system.

When we read the gospels, we realize Jesus usually went to those who were considered outcasts in their society: prostitutes, tax gatherers, women, children, lepers, the blind, and those who were demon possessed. Of all the people who were considered unacceptable, foreigners were at the top of the list. In first century Palestine, Jews steered clear of Gentiles—at least, all Jews but Jesus. John tells us that Jesus went out of His way to meet a Gentile woman who was drawing water from a well in the middle of the day because she wasn't accepted even among other Gentiles. She had married and divorced multiple times, and we can imagine that those relationships probably overlapped. Even among outcasts, she was an outcast. But Jesus found her and struck up a conversation with her. The disciples couldn't believe it. They watched from a distance. When Jesus came back, they said, "Why in the world are You talking to that woman? Not only is she a woman who has been married multiple times . . . she's a Samaritan—and we hate those people! Jesus, don't You know where You are and who You're talking to?"

God has a way of revealing our hearts. He often nudges self-righteous, critical, arrogant people to show His love to the disadvantaged and despised. And it's not good enough to throw a few dollars at them or spend a few minutes taking them food or clothes. He wants to change our hearts so we genuinely love these people! These nudges are some of the most challenging we'll ever experience, but they put us in touch with Jesus' heart like nothing else.

If we're obedient, we'll see God do amazing things in us and through us.

Who are the outcasts who cross your path? Most of the time, we avoid those people. In fact, we've moved into neighborhoods and communities so we don't have to rub shoulders with them. But somehow, God has a way of bringing them into our lives. Are there people you try to avoid? If there are, maybe God is nudging you to show love to them.

Not only will God lead you to people you may not want to talk to, but delivery requests can also come at odd times. I've experienced God Nudges when I had no concept of His presence. In fact, some have come in the middle of the night. God has awakened me to give me a message to deliver, and I've responded, "Can we talk about this later? I want to sleep, Lord."

God's voice may come at anytime. We can't schedule Him on our calendars at our convenience. We may sense His leading while we're at our child's ballgame, at the grocery store, or in the middle of a meeting. If we're obedient, we'll see God do amazing things in us and through us.

What does all this mean? We need to see people the way God sees them. For this to happen, we have to take off our "preferred people" sunglasses. There is no prejudice in the heart of God. He loves everyone. When our hearts beat with His, we begin to care for those He loves—especially the ones who aren't naturally attractive to us.

We have to be careful though, and remember that we're not primarily serving people—we're serving God. If we love and give and serve to win approval, we'll be bitterly disappointed, and we will fizzle out. Loving those who are different from us—socially, economically, ethnically, nationally, and religiously—is incredibly challenging but wonderfully thrilling. It forces us to dig deep, and it allows us to sense God's heart of grace for people we might have laughed at or walked by without a thought. Our focus needs to remain on God. Paul told us:

> "Whatever you do, work at it with all your heart, as working for the Lord, not for human masters, since you know that you will receive an inheritance from the Lord as a reward. It is the Lord Christ you are serving." (Colossians 3:23-24)

If you get connected with God's heart, God's purpose, and God's Spirit so that you minister to people outside your comfort zone, you'll experience His power and love like never before. Are you prepared for the moment when God's agenda collides with your agenda? It will. You can count on it. To respond to God Nudges and become His delivery system, you need to make two crucial commitments:

—You've got to say, "Lord, here am I. Send me."

—And you also have to say, "Lord, I'm Yours. I'm willing to go to anyone, anywhere, anytime."

The Surprise Nudge

I went to college primarily to make money. Our family had eight kids, and my father didn't make much money. Financially, we were always on the edge. I knew I didn't want to live like that for the rest of my life, and I thought a college degree would help me become successful.

In college, I joined a group of students in a Bible study. One day, the leader of the group told me, "Mike, I think the Lord wants you to preach."

I wanted to say, "Get behind me, Satan!" But I just laughed and told him he didn't know what he was talking about. My Mom had told me for years that I was going to be a preacher, and I had ignored her. After all, every preacher I'd ever known was poor, so I was sure I didn't want to become one!

This young man was certain he had received a God Nudge, so he came back the next week and announced boldly, "Mike, you need to listen. I really think the Lord wants you to be a preacher."

This time, I was fierce and firm. I told him bluntly, "Look, I ain't going to be a preacher. They're always broke, and I have no intention of being broke. Besides, preachers drive old rust buckets for cars. Surely God's got something better for me than that!"

As far as I was concerned, the matter was closed. I continued to attend the group, but I wasn't open to any input from the leader. Every time he headed my way, I just shook my head at him. That stopped him before he said a word.

Our group used to serve in little churches around the area. We cleaned kitchens and lobbies, cut grass, trimmed hedges, picked up trash, built things, passed out meals, and helped in any way we could. One day, the leader of our group scheduled a service at a little church in Maypearl, Texas. He came up behind me the next week, and before I could shake my head at him, he said, "Mike, we have a service out at Maypearl next weekend. I told the preacher that you're speaking."

I turned and glared at him, "Listen, I ain't speaking. I don't roll like that. I'll go to Maypearl, fix things, and do carpentry work for them, but I don't have anything to say."

He smirked as he was walking away. "Do what you want to, but when 11 o'clock next Sunday morning rolls around, you're going to be really embarrassed if you don't have something to say to the people at that church."

Later that week, I was reading in Proverbs, and a passage jumped off the page. I thought to myself, "That's a pretty cool verse. I'd better write it down and put it in my pocket—just in case somebody asks me to say something."

The next Sunday in Maypearl, it was announced that I was delivering the message. I got up on the stage. I read the verse from Proverbs, talked about 10 minutes, and then asked, "Does anybody want to get saved?"

Three people got saved that morning. That was pretty cool.

After I walked out of that service, the Lord nudged me and said, "Mike, this is what you're supposed to do." Over the next few months, I still resisted God's leading, but I had the unmistakable sense that God was, in fact, nudging me to become a pastor. I had plenty of reasons to say "No," but the leading of God was clear ... finally, I chose to be obedient to Him. It all began, however, when a young man in a campus Bible study was obedient to a God Nudge and spoke a word to me. Even when I was rude to him, he persisted. Even when I resisted God, He persisted. I soon realized that God's claim on my life isn't about my comfort, reputation, and wealth—it's about His grace and His kingdom.

Have you sensed a collision between your agenda and God's? Don't despair. It's a normal part of the process of learning to walk with Him. Are you avoiding a God Nudge by refusing to listen? Was there a nudge in the past that you neglected or resisted? Maybe it's time to wake it up again and respond in faith. It's never too late to begin again. Even if the old nudge is long past, there's another one just around the corner. Be open, be sensitive to God's Spirit, and be obedient to whatever He tells you to do. There's no greater joy than being a sharp tool in God's gracious hands.

Think about it...

1. Which of the wrong assumptions in this chapter, if any, has been a problem for you? How has it affected your willingness to respond to God?

2. What are some common distractions that keep us from responding to a nudge from God?

3. Do you agree or disagree with the idea that God's agenda is often very different from ours? What kind of collisions of preferences and values do we experience when we respond to God? How can we learn to be more open to His leading?

4. Are there nudges you've neglected or avoided? What would it take for you to respond in faith to them now?

Chapter 3

Escaping Ordinary

When I became a Christian, I didn't understand the kind of people God uses. I assumed I wasn't spiritual enough for God to use me. I'd done some bad things in my life and I was ashamed. My painful awareness of my sinful past made it difficult for me to experience the forgiveness of God. Sometimes the past gnaws at you.

One day, I was repenting for a sin that had haunted me for a long time. I'd probably repented for it at least a hundred times. The sin had happened before I got saved, but I couldn't get it out of my mind. As I prayed, the Lord asked me a question, "What are you talking about? I don't remember that sin at all."

Suddenly, I realized I'd read passages that promised God's complete forgiveness, and I felt so relieved. King David had committed adultery and murder. On top of that, he was a lousy father. If anyone had a reason to wallow in shame, he did! But he wrote:

> "For as high as the heavens are above the earth,
> so great is His love for those who fear Him;
> as far as the east is from the west,
> so far has He removed our transgressions from us."
> (Psalm 103:11-12)

John promised, "If we confess our sins, [God] is faithful and just and will forgive our sins and purify us from all unrighteousness." (1 John 1:9) And God promised, "For I will forgive their wickedness and will remember their sins no more." (Hebrews 8:12)

Of course, God is omniscient. He knows everything that has ever been and ever will be. This passage means He chooses not to remember our sins against us in any way. Once we have asked for forgiveness, God graciously forgives our sins, but our human nature doesn't allow us to forget. Some of us have a terrible blend of tender hearts and haunted memories, and we're plagued with guilt. Until we understand and experience God's grace, we're in trouble.

The Swap

We struggle with guilt as long as we think we have to earn God's love by being "good enough". The gospel of grace loudly proclaims that we'll never be good enough to gain leverage with God. It's a hopeless proposition. Our only hope is that Jesus loves us, forgives us, and accepts us based on His righteousness instead of ours. Paul described an incredible swap in a letter to the Corinthians:

> "God made Him who had no sin to be sin for us,
> so that in Him we might become the righteousness
> of God." (2 Corinthians 5:21)

Do you see it? He takes our sin, and He clothes us in Christ's righteousness. This is the wonderful, life-changing news that's the subject of the great hymns and songs of the faith. It's the source of breath-taking amazement that God would go to such lengths to forgive and accept people like you and I. Our qualification isn't because we've met God's standard, but because Jesus has. We aren't secure because of our good works, but because of His righteousness. When we grasp the incredible swap of our sins for Christ's righteousness, we can relax, but we also become highly motivated to please the one who rescued us. We want to honor Him in every possible way! We want God to use us.

I too, have also struggled with the worry that I'm not smart enough to be used of God. Throughout my years in school, I sat in Bible classes and chapels hearing some of the greatest preachers in the nation. Often, I was in awe of them and thought, *Man, I'd give anything to be that sharp!* And just as often, I heard another voice in my head whispering, "You could never be like that. He's way out of your league." I was filled with self-doubt and anxiety. I was sure I'd never be the man God wanted me to be. I asked some of these preachers to pray for me. I hoped a super-saint's prayers would do the trick. I'm sure it helped, but the super-saint status wasn't instantly accessed. I wasted a lot of time (mine and theirs) in this futile pursuit. Then I realized we're all just ordinary people in a relationship of grace with an extraordinary God.

> *God is looking for available, faithful, responsive people.*

The most significant thing about us isn't that we're beautiful or plain, smart or dull, tall or short, rich or poor, articulate or mumbling. No, the most important fact is that we've been born into God's family, and He has a magnificent plan for each of us. His purposes are far above anything we can imagine, and He has chosen us to be His partners in the greatest adventure the world has ever known. When we compare ourselves with others, we can always find somebody who has more talents or experiences than we have. God isn't looking for the finest talents. He's looking for available, faithful, responsive people. Paul put it this way:

"For we are God's handiwork, created in Christ Jesus

to do good works, which God prepared in advance for us to do." (Ephesians 2:10)

Training Camp

The Bible often uses agricultural metaphors to describe our lives of faith. Plants grow strong and fruitful only when they get plenty of sunshine, water, and nutrients. Many Christians aren't growing because they're living in a spiritual desert! We need to find churches where we get plenty of good teaching, encouragement, and vision. The church is where dreams of being used by God can be nourished.

Before I was born again, I used to think church was for weak people. It's not. The church is a training camp for God's warriors! In fact, everything good that has ever happened to me has happened in church. Church has been my saving station and my feeding station. I've seen God transform countless lives, but almost always in the context of a local body of believers. We're called "the body of Christ," and we need each other to function well. In these strong, supportive relationships, an ordinary person can be trained and motivated to do extraordinary things. Church is where I get God's "super" to come down on my "natural"!

I really don't know how much time I have left on this planet, but I'm trying to live life to the fullest. I need the love, stimulation, and challenge of the body of Christ so I can be most effective for Him.

Willing

In the book of Acts, Luke tells the exciting story of the development of the church after Jesus ascended to heaven. By the middle of the story, Paul and Barnabas were in the city of Lystra, and they saw a man who was crippled in both of his feet (Acts 14:8-20). He had been an invalid since birth. He was in the crowd listening to Paul preach about Jesus, and Paul noticed him. In fact, when Paul looked at him, he saw that the man had faith. At that moment, Paul had a God Nudge. He told the crippled man, "Stand up on your feet." The man jumped up and began to walk. The crowd went crazy! They instantly assumed the miracle meant Barnabas and Paul were Roman gods who had come down from heaven. They thought Barnabas was Zeus and Paul was Hermes. The crowd wanted to kill bulls and offer sacrifices to them. If anyone ever wanted the praise of people, this was it! But Paul knew his rightful place. He told the crowd, "Men, why are you doing this? We too are only men, human just like you." Paul and Barnabas refused to take God's place in the minds and hearts of the people they served.

That's a good example for you and I. I'm just an ordinary man, but when the power of God comes upon me, I can do extraordinary things! That's what happened to Paul and Barnabas that day. They were just ordinary men, but they were doing some crazy, extraordinary miracles by the power of God.

A few years ago, I spoke at Grand Rapids First Assembly of God, where my friend, Sam Rijfkogel, is the pastor. While I was preaching, I noticed a young lady on the third row, and I had a God Nudge. I knew she had just come from the hospital because the hospital identification band was still on her wrist. I sensed she needed an extraordinary touch of God that day.

Later, I learned that the young lady's name was Katie. She was a gifted athlete who excelled in volleyball. But when she was in the hospital, the doctors told her that because of the extent of her injuries, she would never play college volleyball again. She was devastated. I listened to God, looked at Katie, and told her, "God said He's going to heal you today."

When I spoke those words to her, it was as though you could see her reach out and latch onto them. She got up out of her seat and walked forward with full faith, believing the words that were spoken in the Spirit to her—and Katie was healed that day! A few weeks later, I received a DVD from Pastor Sam's church. It showed Katie back in the line-up and playing on her college team. What a marvelous thing!

But remember: It wasn't me! Katie's healing didn't have anything to do with me. God was the initiator of the promise and the healer. He's the Alpha and the Omega. Katie had the faith to be healed, and her parents believed God would heal her. I was just the delivery agent who was willing to respond to a God Nudge.

Like Paul and Barnabas, if you want to be used in the extraordinary things of God, you're going to have to live by faith. Notice that both sides need faith: Paul had faith to believe God would heal the crippled man, and the man had faith that God was speaking and working through Paul. In the same way, I had to have a measure of faith to believe God wanted to heal Katie, and she had to respond with great faith.

> *God delights in doing the supernatural - the unusual - miracles no one could imagine.*

Sometimes, God Nudges come with bold commands instead of pastoral tenderness. When Paul saw the crippled man, he didn't enter into a long conversation about his past hurts and current worries. He said simply and boldly, "Stand up on your feet!" Paul didn't sympathize with his pain, and he didn't comfort him in his chaos. He just said to him, "If you want God to do what He's never done before, you're going to have to do something you've never done before." He announced in front of everyone listening: "It's time for you to walk!"

What's the miracle in this story? Is it the fact that the lame man walked? That's certainly a magnificent miracle, but I think there is a greater one here. I think the greater miracle is that a man who had never walked didn't hesitate to do something he'd never done before. God delights in doing the supernatural, the unusual, and the miracles that no one could imagine. He uses ordinary people to do extraordinary things.

I've seen and heard some wonderful stories of God's power unleashed in the lives of people. In the Azusa Street revival, the Spirit touched a young lady who had never learned how to play the piano. She sat down on the bench, and as her fingers glided over the ivory keyboard, you would have thought she'd been playing all her life. Missionaries who had never learned foreign languages began speaking fluently by the Spirit. With this God-given skill, they were able to preach to people in their own languages. Now, that's extraordinary!

Some of us read these accounts and conclude, "That's great, but I'm out. I don't have the gift of working miracles, and my faith is too small." Miracles happen when ordinary people trust an extraordinary God. If you see yourself ordinary, you're a good candidate to be used by God.

But we need a word of caution: We need to be sure to put the glory in the right place. The people in Lystra assumed Paul and Barnabas were gods, and today, some Christians assume that those who trust God for great things are "super saints." They're not. They're just normal people with faith in a God who is far beyond the norm. If people promote themselves instead of God, be cautious about trusting them, and pray for them. If you call attention to yourself instead of giving God glory for working through you, get on your knees and ask God to forgive you and change your heart. Self-glory is destructive and evil. Paul knew that if they made gods out of him and Barnabas, the praise would eventually destroy them. Paul had it right: He was well aware that he was just an ordinary person whom God used to do an extraordinary thing.

Sensitive

We don't have to be sinless, brilliant or supremely gifted to be used by God, and to be part of His delivery system. We do, however, have to be available, and we also need to develop sensitivity to the Spirit's whisper. It's easy to miss it. Learning to listen is one of the most important elements of our walks with God. Sensitivity usually comes with practice.

I've always approached preaching the Bible with the utmost respect. Whether I'm preaching to four people or four thousand people, I prepare the same way. My routine consists of ferocious study and fervent prayer. Years ago at a pastor's conference, Ed Young asked Bishop T.D. Jakes, "How do you prepare to preach the gospel?"

Bishop Jakes smiled and replied, "I study myself full, I think myself clear, I pray myself hot, and then I let myself go." That's a great recipe to be used of God—for a pastor or for any of us.

For many years, I've made a commitment to spend time every day in prayer. In this give-and-take communication with God, He prepares my spirit to be useful to Him. In Revelation, John wrote, "He who has an ear, let him hear what the Spirit says to the church" (Revelation 3:13). God is speaking, but some of us aren't listening. It's as if we're tuned to an AM station when God is speaking on FM. We're finite, and we're in a relationship with the Infinite, so it's easy to misunderstand Him. To keep lines of communication clear, I've determined to work on my tuning to clear away all the static. I'm committed to be on the right channel, and I'm going to keep my antennae up and working, because

I want to hear what the Spirit has to say to me.

Our church has multiple services every weekend. Before I preach, I whisper this prayer:

> "Lord, open my eyes to see and my ears to hear, and give my heart the ability to discern what Your desire is for each of the people here in front of me today. And lastly Lord, give me the courage to step out in faith when I receive a God Nudge from heaven."

I'm God's servant and God's vessel. I want Him to use me any way He chooses to deliver His message to the people He loves.

A Wake-up Call

Many years ago while I was attending a chapel service at the Bible College in Waxahachie, Texas, a missionary in Arkansas described how the Lord woke him up about 2:00 a.m. on a cold winter night. The Lord gave him a vision of a family in a van that was a few miles away. The missionary sensed the Lord wanted him to go help this family. He got dressed, got in his car, and drove down the road in the direction the Lord impressed him to go. About thirty miles down the road, he found a family stranded by the side of the road in a van. He stopped and helped them get home.

As he was driving back to his house, he began to talk to the Lord about the incident. He asked the Lord a question: "Lord, why did You have me do that? I'm thirty miles away and I know of a lot of godly people between my house and where this vehicle was stranded. Why did You choose me? Why couldn't You use one of these other Christians around here?"

The Lord answered, "You're right. I have plenty of people between you and the stranded family. I woke two other people, but they refused the God Nudge. You were the third one I called, and you answered."

This story makes me wonder how many God Nudges I neglect because I want another hour of sleep or I think what I'm doing is more important than God's leading. I want to be sensitive to God and available to respond to His voice. I'm sure you do, too.

GOD CAN USE ANYONE

As a general principle, God uses people with humble, tender hearts and courageous faith. He speaks to us as Spirit-filled believers, but He also nudges people who aren't Spirit-filled. And in fact, His grace is so great that He sometimes uses people who aren't even walking with Him. The Scriptures are full of God using flawed people. If He tried to use anyone else, He'd run out of resources pretty quickly! We know Abraham as "the father of our faith," but he lied about his wife and showed a remarkable lack of courage at some points. Jacob was one of the patriarchs, but he was a serial deceiver until he wrestled with God.

> *God uses people with humble, tender hearts and courageous faith.*

When Samuel was a little boy, his mother, Hannah, fulfilled a vow and gave him to Eli the priest to be raised in the temple (1 Samuel 1-3). The boy lived in the house of the Lord, but he had never heard the voice of the Lord. One night, the Lord spoke to Samuel, but he was confused. He thought Eli was calling him. Eli wasn't a good example of a father or a spiritual leader, but he finally realized God was speaking to the boy. After the third time

Samuel reported hearing a voice, Eli told him,

> "Go and lie down, and if He calls you, say, 'Speak, Lord, for your servant is listening.'" (1 Samuel 3:9)

In the same way, many of us are like Samuel. We regularly go to the Lord's house, but we don't readily recognize His voice.

Quite often, we don't listen until we're in trouble—and sometimes, big trouble. When I was a boy, my father had a truck driving business. He passed away when I was 17, so I took over his business hauling fruit across the state of Texas. I also trucked Christmas trees out of New Mexico and peaches out of Colorado. In the middle of the night on a 500-mile trip, I was driving into Caprock, Texas, when the engine stopped running. It quit right in the middle of the freeway. I didn't know what to do. I tried to maneuver the truck and trailer off to the side of the road, but I was going up a hill, so I couldn't go very far. The truck came to a slow stop. I sat there for a minute trying to figure out what I was going to do, when I remembered that I'd started straight-shift cars by rolling them down hills and popping the clutch. Maybe that would work for this truck. I let the truck roll backward down the hill and let off the clutch, but nothing happened. The truck had no power. No matter what I tried, it wasn't going to start. (Later I would discover there was a short in a wire.) But I had made a big mistake by rolling it backward. When I did, the trailer swerved out into the traffic and crossed both lanes of the highway! My truck had jackknifed. I got out and peered at my predicament: I was stuck across the highway, in the middle of the night, with no lights, no power, and no flares to warn oncoming traffic that my truck and trailer was sprawled across two lanes of traffic. Fortunately, there wasn't much traffic out in west Texas.

I was only 17 years old and as far away from God as I could

be. I knew about God, but I didn't have a relationship with Him. While growing up, my Mom had a drug problem—she drug me to the church every Sunday. Like Samuel, I'd grown up in the house of God, but I knew Him only from a distance.

As I sat in the truck that night, I began to pray because I needed God's help. I whispered a simple prayer: "Jesus, save me." I can't explain it, but after three or four minutes of having a truck jackknifed in the middle of the freeway, something miraculous happened: The engine started up! I pulled it off the side of the road, and then it died again. That night, I realized God had heard my simple prayer.

But, you may ask, how could God hear a prayer of someone who wasn't born again? I believe He does. Two things helped me out that night:

—Many people had been praying for me. In fact, if it weren't for my mom and my family members praying for me, I wouldn't be where I am today. I've ridden on their prayers.

—I sensed the incredible love that God has for each of us. God shows His love to people even before they actually trust in Him. Theologians call it "prevenient grace"—the grace that comes before we're saved. Even when I was sinning, God helped me get a jackknifed truck out of the road. His answer to my prayer kept me from killing myself and killing other people that night.

Too often, we focus our attention on our needs, our plans, and our goals, and we hope God will make us happy and successful. Being self-absorbed isn't a life of real faith. It's not about us at all. God's grace reaches into the lives of the hurting, the needy, and the broken—and He delights in revealing Himself to them. It's not called "amazing grace" for nothing. It's extraordinary!

Think about it...

1. What are some reasons why people may feel disqualified or "less than" they need to be in order to be used by God? Have you ever felt that way?

2. What truths and promises give us peace and confidence that God has qualified us to become useful to Him?

3. How can prayer, Bible study, and talks with mature, trusted Christian friends help us become more sensitive to the Spirit's whispers?

4. Does it encourage you or deflate you to realize that God uses ordinary people to accomplish extraordinary things for His kingdom? Explain your answer.

Chapter 4

Learning to Discern

I'm convinced that all real Christians have an innate desire to communicate with God. Many believers, however, have never been exposed to people who operate in the gifts of the Spirit. No matter what our spiritual background may be, all of us need to learn to detect the voice of God. We need training and experience to notice God Nudges.

Stop, Look, and Listen

Karen and I have had the privilege of pastoring three churches, and each of them has had a unique touch of God. He works in and through each church in slightly different ways. To get in step with the Spirit, we have to slow down, notice what God is doing, and catch the wave of the Spirit.

At every church service, I usually greet people as they come in. I shake hands with them, look in their eyes, and listen to them talk. My strategy is to "Stop, Look, and Listen." Many of the people who walk in our doors have been asking God to do something in their lives or in the lives of those they love. Before they darken the doors of the church, they've been praying a lot! And many people believe God for a miracle. All week, my team and I have asked God to answer those prayers. In fact, some of the people who come are truly desperate. They're on their last shred of hope. They may have prayed, "How long, Lord? How much longer must I live with this cancer?" "When are You going to help me with my business?" "What is the combination that will unlock my child's salvation . . . or give direction for her future?" "Lord, will you help me have a child?" "Father, what can I do about my son's addiction?" These aren't flippant prayers. These people have been storming the gates of heaven, but so far, they haven't received an answer.

After shaking a few hands, I often stand against the back wall of the church. I stretch out my hand over the congregation, and I pray for God to perform the miraculous. After two or three songs in the service, I stop talking to people. I then look around at the crowd and pray for them. All the while, I'm listening to what the Holy Spirit may be saying to me, to someone in the congregation, and to our church.

> *Spiritual gifts are not dependent on natural talents and intelligence.*

While I'm praying for people, the Spirit may give me an image or a sentence about a particular person. I know it's the Holy Spirit because I'm usually not aware of what's going on in the person's life. And I know it's not a result of being the smartest guy in the room. Spiritual gifts aren't dependent on natural talents and intelligence.

Has that happened to you? A thought popped up in your mind and you think, "Man, I'm really smart." But then you got a grip on yourself, and you quickly recognize, "I know it must be the Holy Spirit because I couldn't have come up with it on my own."

It's exhilarating to operate in the gifts. We have to develop a deep sense of humility: It's from God, to God, and for God—it's not about us. Even the apostle Paul, the greatest leader of the church, admitted, "I know in part and I prophesy in part," and "We see through a glass dimly" (1 Corinthians 13:9,12). When God initially gives me a nudge about someone, I seldom understand very clearly. I see only partially and dimly, but I'm confident God sees in 3D.

When God puts someone on my heart, I try to spend time with

that person to pray, talk, and discern what God wants to say. I don't want to be presumptuous and jump to a wrong conclusion!

When we're moving from the seen to the unseen worlds, we can mess up. I try to spend undistracted time with the person, ask questions, and listen to the Holy Spirit as we talk. Quite often, the conversation reveals hidden hurts and hopes that give a lot of insight about the person's needs.

When we read the gospels, we marvel at Jesus' power to heal the sick, cleanse lepers, restore sight to the blind, raise the dead back to life, cast out demons, still storms, and perform many other kinds of miracles. However, we need to see the broader picture. Matthew observed,

> "Jesus went about teaching, preaching and healing all manner of sickness." (Matthew 9:35)

Did you catch the sequence? He taught and preached to them before He healed them.

Almost every time I get an impression about someone, I don't take action or announce the word until I've preached God's Word. It amazes me how many things the Holy Spirit reveals to me during a dynamic worship service. Often, I understand much more after worship and preaching than I did before. At one point in His ministry, Jesus rebuked people because they insisted on Him giving them a prophetic word. He told them to read their Bible—that's the reliable source of prophetic words!

A pastor recently told his congregation, "I have a word for every one of you in this service. It's a word from God." Then he instructed them to open up their Bibles to any passage, familiar or unfamiliar. He explained, "That's a word from the Lord. It is a word from the Lord because the Bible is God's Word."

God Nudges are wonderful events in the life of an individual and the corporate life of a church, but we can't live on them alone. We have to feast on God's truth in the Bible: read it, study it, pray over it, and apply it. Let it inspire you, correct you, and direct you. Every single word in the Bible is the inspired Word of God.

We can't orchestrate God Nudges. Sometimes, they come in bunches, but at other times, very few occur for a period of time. Maybe people pray more at some points, perhaps they expect God to speak to them, or maybe spiritual conflict has something to do with it. But maybe God simply has His sovereign, divine reasons and seasons to accomplish His will. We don't have to know why He does what He does. We only need to acknowledge that He's infinitely wise, good, and strong. We can trust Him.

Three Voices

At any point in time, I can hear three voices inside my head: my voice, God's voice, and the devil's voice. One of those three voices is always talking to me, and sometimes, it's two or all three. Because they sound like my own voice, I can easily confuse them. It's important to distinguish between them. Jesus said, "My sheep hear My voice, and I know them, and they follow Me." (John 10:27 NKJV)

> *One of the biggest obstacles is our culture's addiction to speed and busyness.*

How do I distinguish the voice of God? I have to spend time with God to learn to sense His nudge, hear His voice, and distinguish His voice from the others. The more time we spend with God, the clearer His voice becomes, and the more our spirit becomes attuned to the Holy Spirit. It's like our antenna gets stronger and its reception is better. One of the biggest obstacles is our culture's addiction to speed and busyness. We are always in motion, and we think there's something terribly wrong when we're quiet and still. Author Richard Foster observed, "Our adversary majors in three things: noise, hurry and crowds. If he can keep us engaged in 'muchness' and 'manyness,' he will rest satisfied."[2]

More than ever before, Christians need to slow down and listen to God's voice. In the opening chapters of Luke's Gospel, we find a man who learned how to wait on the Lord and pay attention to His nudges. Luke tells us about Simeon:

> "Now there was a man in Jerusalem called Simeon, who was righteous and devout. He was waiting for the consolation of Israel, and the Holy Spirit was upon him. It had been revealed to him by the Holy Spirit that he would not die before he had seen the Lord's Christ. Moved by the Spirit, he went into the temple courts. When the parents brought in the child Jesus to do for Him what the custom of the Law required, Simeon took Him in his arms and praised God, saying: 'Sovereign Lord, as You have promised, You now dismiss Your servant in peace. For my eyes have seen Your salvation, which You have prepared in the sight of all people, a light for revelation to the Gentiles and for glory to Your people Israel.' The child's father and mother marveled at what was said about Him. Then Simeon blessed them and said to Mary, His mother: 'This child is destined to cause the falling and rising of many in Israel, and to be a sign that will be spoken against, so that the thoughts

---

[2]Richard Foster, (1988) *Celebration of Discipline,* SanFrancisco, Harper

> of many hearts will be revealed. And a sword will pierce your own soul too.' " (Luke 2:25-38)

Simeon heard the voice of the Lord. He wasn't preoccupied with all the other voices that were going on in his life. He learned to drown out those other voices that were yelling at him or whispering to him. And Simeon wasn't in a hurry. He had a God Nudge, but He waited for God to show him the answer to his prayers. Finally, he had the thrill of holding the Messiah in his arms.

We need to understand what was going on in this story. Simeon's patient waiting was remarkable. At the beginning of the gospel accounts of Christ's life, the Jewish people had experienced about 400 years of silence since Malachi put down his pen. There were few words from God, and very few nudges. Simeon grew up in a time that was spiritually dark and dim in Israel's history. Some ancient writings suggest he was 113 years old when we meet him in Luke's Gospel. He had a sense from God that "the consolation of Israel," the promised Messiah, would be born in his lifetime—but time was running out! Simeon was a man with unbroken focus. He finally witnessed what he had been promised. He had listened, waited, and trusted God to come through in His way and in His timing. Simeon is a wonderful example for us.

How many of us would have bailed out long before that precious moment? We live in a microwave/drive-thru culture. We expect God to answer our prayers—now! We hate any delays. If we learn to wait, we'll experience richness in our relationship with God, and we'll see Him work in wonderful ways.

I know a minister who stayed up all night to help a young college man be delivered of demon possession. The young man had lost his mind and speech. After many, many hours of patiently working with the young man, he was freed and got his mind and speech back. Afterwards, Norvel Hayes was commenting on what had happened. He said something that has stuck with me. "Many will never be able to do what I did simply because they haven't the patience. You need to ask God to give you the gift of patience, if you want to do the works that Jesus did."

Simeon had a deep, passionate reverence for God. If we want to hear the voice of the Lord, we can't be superficial, part-time, lukewarm Christians. We have to dive deep into the waters of God's love, be amazed by His infinite power, and find our sense of identity and strength in Him alone. In our culture, there aren't many people who are "sold out" to Jesus. In fact, many people who attend church look down their noses and ridicule people who are passionate about God's "crazy love." People who want to know Him, love Him, and honor Him aren't normal according to the world's standards, but they're right in line with God's design for every one of His children. Radical love and obedience are "the normal Christian life."

The Holy Spirit led Simeon to the temple that day. He had learned to live according to a biblical principle: Devotional people move with destiny in mind. They're constantly whispering a prayer, "Lord, what do you have for me today?" Devotional people are sensitive to the Spirit's nudges, but they wait on the Lord before they make a major decision. The psalmist described the results of failing to be sensitive to God:

> "They soon forgot what the Lord had done and did not wait for His counsel. In the desert they gave in to cravings; in the wastelands, they put God to the test. So God gave them what they asked for, but sent leanness to their soul." (Psalm 106:13-15)

When we forget God, our selfish desires dominate our minds and hearts. We may get what we want, but it ruins our lives. All day, every day, people pursue popularity, possessions, and positions. They think these things can fill the emptiness in their hearts, but they can't. Only God can. They may achieve their goals, but their pursuits turn into dust and ashes. Simeon wasn't that kind of man, and I'm not that kind of man. I don't want "leanness in my soul" because I've pursued worthless things. The urgent is not always the important, but the important is always urgent.

When Simeon arrived at the temple that day, he didn't realize his prayers were finally going to be answered—he was going to dedicate the Lord Jesus Christ. It was the eighth day, the day when parents brought baby boys to be dedicated to the Lord. Simeon sensed that this child, Mary's boy, was the Messiah, the Lamb of God who would take away the sins of the world! Can you imagine the thrill? But it wouldn't have happened if he hadn't been sensitive to the Spirit and then patiently waited for the Lord's answer.

Distractions can come at any moment as we try to listen to the Lord.

Distractions can come at any moment as we try to listen to the Lord. In my years of sensing God Nudges, I've learned that when God is just about to speak to me, I'll get a phone call, a text message, or an email that seems urgent. If I'm not careful, I'll get distracted and miss what the Lord has for me. I've also noticed that when I pray, the first few minutes are often crowded with thoughts of a hundred things I have to do. To get ahead of these distractions, I take my daily planner into the prayer room so I can write down everything I have to do that day. Before I pray (or as I begin praying), I list every responsibility and meeting for the day. By the time I'm done, the enemy doesn't have any ammunition left, and I can pray more intently about the things God puts on my heart. My mind is clear and my Spirit is open.

We are human "beings," not human "doings." We can get so busy doing things that we forget to be thoroughly human—listening, caring, and responding to God and other people.

Listening is part work, part art, and part science. Discerning the voice of the Lord has everything to do with the right timing. Our human brain is able to hear about 1800 words a minute. The most articulate speaker can only speak about 350 words per minute. In a discussion with a spouse or a child, in a meeting at work, or while we're sitting in a church service, we can hear three or four conversations at the same time.

We don't pay equal attention to every voice we hear. For example, a police officer can pull us over, and he instantly has 100 percent of our attention. But when a teenager is told to clean up his room, the message doesn't even make a dent. However, if he's threatened with consequences, the applied pressure often produces more acute listening. Rewards and consequences heighten the intensity of our listening. When we're convinced things count, we pay attention.

Simeon was a devout man, a devotional man, and a discerning man. He loved God with all his heart, developed a deep walk with God, and discerned the voice of God—and he responded in faith. As we follow his example, we'll learn to distinguish between God's voice, our own voice of selfish desires, and the devil's voice. How do we know it's God's voice speaking to us? Ask a few pertinent questions:

1. Does it line up with His Word?

A word from the Lord will never contradict the truth of the Bible.

2. Does it honor Jesus?

Everything that I do, everything that I hear from the Holy Spirit will honor Jesus.

3. Does it help somebody?

God has a heart for the hurting and a desire to reach out to mankind. I know it's God if it's going to help somebody, because that's the nature of God.

THE VOICE OF GOD

When God Nudges us, He never speaks in a voice that accuses, condemns, or tempts us to sin. You can count on it! I've heard negative, destructive messages spoken by Christians, and sometimes even from pulpits. It's a shame and a tragedy. God's grace, love, and forgiveness are the primary messages God gives us to speak to those in need. It's the gospel of grace, and people never get tired of hearing it! I don't have to point out their sin to them. The Holy Spirit will do that as I talk about Christ. I don't have to make them conform to the Ten Commandments or the Sermon on the Mount. It's the Spirit's job to awaken hearts and motivate people to live for God. The message of Jesus is that we're so bad it took the death of the Son of God to pay for our sins, but He loves so much He was glad to die for us. That message is liberating and inspiring!

Another mark of God's grace is that He's willing to repeat His message to us over and over again. Look at the disciples: They were slow to understand Jesus' message and purpose, and we're not that different from them! God often speaks to me more than once. If I'm sitting in a service, or even if I'm at a coffee shop, and I get a God Nudge for somebody, I often notice, but go about my business. If the impression comes back a second time, then I begin to believe the clue may be the voice of God.

How do I discern if it's my voice? My voice usually wants me to get all the glory, win at all costs, hide from risk, or further my reputation. Pride is a powerful but sometimes subtle problem. We can say that we're doing something to honor God, but under the surface, we want to bask in the glow of admiration for being such "a good Christian" or "a wonderful leader," or having "a sensitive heart." We can even deceive ourselves to think our motives are pure. God spoke through Jeremiah to warn the people, "Should you then seek great things for yourself? Do not seek them." (Jeremiah 45:5) Don't be surprised when the Lord shows you that an action you've taken had ulterior, selfish motives. We all have them, but not all of us recognize them and have the humility to repent.

I've given God Nudges to people who have done the unthinkable. Some have committed horrible sins and crimes, but God loves all people, and He wants to do great things in their lives. I don't blast people about their sins. People are hard enough on themselves without me piling on. They don't need my voice to help condemn them. They need my voice to talk about a future, a hope, and a life they can have in Jesus Christ.

How can we recognize the devil's voice? It is a pride voice: "Go pull that person out of the wheelchair and people will see how great you are." His message goes against God's Word. It harshly accuses us: "You're so stupid! God could never use anybody like you!" It condemns: "You blew it again. Look at all the sins you've committed. Do you really think God would answer your prayers?" And it tempts us to commit a wide variety of sins, including jealousy, bitterness, lust, drunkenness, and many others. When we hear this seductive voice, it often says, "Don't worry, nobody will see you. And besides, it's not hurting anybody."

A friend told me that the Lord speaks to him in threes. If he hears a particular word from God three times, then he knows it's from God. Twice seems to be enough for me, but if I hear it three times, it's an added benefit. Actually, I'm often suspicious of the messages that come to me. If I wait, and if I trust God to repeat them, God is gracious to validate His nudges. The enemy of our souls isn't very patient. He may tempt me once, and if I don't give in, he gives up on me. But if God wants something to happen, He gives me multiple nudges to confirm His message. That's the way it works with me.

On many occasions, I only receive a person's name or face. I seldom get a full message to share with someone. When I get a partial message about people, I tell them, "I feel like God wants me to pray for you." I can make this statement in front of a thousand people and feel completely comfortable. Then, when I step through the door of prayer, God often gives me the second part. If nothing specific comes to mind, I start asking questions. I'll ask, "Why do you think the Lord put you on my heart today?" Or I may ask, "What do you need from the Lord?" When I hear them share their hearts, I can discern what's really going on. The insight may happen in a flash, or it may take a while. It doesn't matter. Time isn't the issue. I'm not in a hurry. I want to be faithful, persistent, and sensitive to God and to the person. Peppered in the conversation are many silent prayers. I ask, "Lord, what are You trying to say to us here?" Quite often, He answers to provide the insight we need so we can trust Him to meet a specific, previously hidden need.

Mentors

Have you sensed a God Nudge lately? If not, or if you're confused about the message you've sensed from God, or if you're having trouble distinguishing the three voices, find someone who is skilled and experienced in God Nudges. For years, I've spent time with pastors, lay leaders, preachers, and evangelists who are sensitive to the gifts of the Spirit. From them, I've learned how to discern the voice of the Lord.

I have a friend whose father is a powerful, healing evangelist. I asked my friend, "How did you learn to discern the voice of the Lord, and how is He using you?"

He gave me a surprising answer. He said, "I grew up with it. It's second nature to me."

Sooner or later, I hope God Nudges become second nature to you, too. Put yourself around enough people, in enough services, in enough places that you begin to discern the voice of God. If you're not involved in a church, find one that is Spirit-filled and alive with the love of Jesus. When you spend time immersed in these relationships, you'll learn wonderful lessons, develop listening skills, and become more sensitive to the Spirit of God. God will use you as one of His choice agents on the earth, because He knows that you're willing to be a delivery system to answer people's prayers.

Let me just say a few words about using the God Nudge in church. I have been in a Spirit-filled church for a very long time. Down through the years, we've all seen some pretty strange things done and said in the name of Jesus.

One of the most important things to remember when it comes to acting on a God Nudge, is that 1 Corinthians 14:40 reminds us that all things are to be done decently and in order.

A friend of mine had been a part of a small non-denominational church for some time, when a woman began attending who, obviously, was from a more Pentecostal background. She was very expressive in her style of worship, and at times, it made other people who were attending the church uncomfortable. She was positive that her style of worship was more acceptable to

God than what was being done in the church, so she would constantly approach the Pastor after service and tell him, "God told me to tell you … that you need to use more gifts of the Spirit throughout the church service." Week after week, the woman would tell the Pastor, "God told me to tell you…" It was beginning to affect others in the church – what she was doing and how she was going about it, was not being done decently and in order.

Finally, my friend couldn't take it anymore. He confronted her, "Diane, God has put our Pastor in a position of authority over this church and all who attend. The way that we worship is the way that has been established by the leadership of this church. You are wrong to keep telling our Pastor that 'God told you to tell him…' to do something different. Don't you think that if God wanted to tell him to do something different, He would tell the Pastor Himself?" Not too long after that, Diane left to find someplace else to worship. She refused to be under the authority of the leadership of that church.

The bottom line is this: Every church has a system. You and I have to understand the culture of the church we are in and fall under its leadership. If the Pastor of the church does not want your brand of being used in the gifts of the Spirit, you need to respect that. God places a Pastor to lead the church and He flows through the leadership.

Our largest weekly attendance this past year was just over six thousand people. Can you imagine the chaos and instability it would bring to the church if every person came up and said to me: "God told me to tell you …"

Think about it…

1. What are some ways you can discern a person's hidden hopes and fears? How can you detect your own?

2. Describe the differences in the three voices: God's, yours, and the devil's.

3. Is busyness a distraction to your ability to listen to God? Why or why not? If it is, what can you do about it?

4. What would it take for God Nudges to become second nature for you?

5. Who can be a mentor for you?

Chapter 5

Overcoming God Nudge Obstacles

Don't be surprised if you resist God Nudges. Some of us resist because we're afraid, others because we're preoccupied, and a few because we feel superior to the people God wants us to reach out and touch. It happens to everybody. In fact, one of the most famous stories in the Bible is about a man who ran—and swam—away from God's prompting.

Dislike Toward Certain People Groups

Jonah was a prophet in Israel who previously had said "Yes" to God. He already agreed to be God's delivery agent, but then God asked him to do something "outside the box." The Lord told Jonah to go to Nineveh to tell them about God's love and strength. But Jonah hated those people. I mean Jonah despised them! They were the al-Qaida of his day—ruthless killers who were sworn enemies of Israel.

But God loves every person in the world, even those who hate Him and His people. And God picked Jonah to tell them the good news of His grace. Jonah, though, wasn't too receptive to this God Nudge!

> "The word of the Lord came to Jonah son of Amittai: 'Go to the great city of Nineveh and preach against it, because its wickedness has come up before me.' But Jonah ran way from the Lord and headed for Tarshish. He went down to Joppa, where he found a ship bound for that port. After paying the fare, he

> went aboard and sailed for Tarshish to flee from the Lord." (Jonah 1:1-3)

God pointed toward Nineveh and told Jonah, "Go over there. Give a message to the people of Nineveh." But instead of paying attending to the nudge God was giving him, Jonah bailed out on God and His mission for him. Basically, he told God, "No chance. I'm going on vacation. In fact, I'm going as far away as possible. Count me out!"

He hopped on a cruise ship out of Joppa and headed the opposite direction. On the sea, Jonah felt like he had dodged a bullet. He had said "No" to God, and now he was safe onboard the ship. Think again, Jonah! Suddenly, a terrible storm began to howl. Fierce winds and huge waves threatened to destroy the ship.

It didn't take the captain and sailors very long to figure it out: Somebody on the boat was the center of God's attention. Finally, Jonah raised his hand and said, "Hey guys, it's me. I'm the disobedient one. God told me to do something, and I'm running from Him." But the prophet had a plan: "You might as well just go ahead and kill me because it isn't going to get any better while I'm alive." That's a pretty depressed prophet, isn't it? The sailors were finished with Jonah, but God wasn't.

> "Then they took Jonah and threw him overboard, and the raging sea grew calm. At this the men greatly feared the Lord, and they offered a sacrifice to the Lord and made vows to Him. But the Lord provided a great fish to swallow Jonah, and Jonah was inside the fish three days and three nights." (Jonah 1:15-17)

After they threw Jonah overboard, nobody knew what happened to him. He vanished in the waves. Three days later, he appeared on the beach, but he was a changed man. Physically, he looked different. When the great fish swallowed him, the acid in its stomach bleached his dark skin snow white. In the fish's stomach, he had lost a lot of strength— there was nothing good to eat in there! As he walked from the shore to the great city of Nineveh, he looked like a white scarecrow!

But something else had changed: Jonah's heart. At some point during those three days, he finally responded to God, "Okay, I get the message!" Jonah was ready to obey God. Always patient and persistent with people like Jonah, you and I, God sent His word to him again to tell him to go to Nineveh. I can just hear Jonah saying, "Yes, sir. This time I'm ready to go!"

Nineveh was one of the largest, richest cities of the ancient world. It took a person three days to walk through it. On the first day there, Jonah began telling the people that in forty days the city and all the people were going to be destroyed by God for their wickedness. When the message made its way to the king, he called for a fast. The king even made the animals fast! In an incredible response to God, 120,000 people repented and turned to the Lord. When God saw they had repented and turned from their evil ways, He had compassion. He didn't destroy them after all.

What a marvelous thing! God responded, "I'm not going to bring destruction on the people of Nineveh because they repented." Repentance saved their skins. They were headed for destruction, but they trusted God for forgiveness and a new direction. What a miracle!

Think about the emotions Jonah probably felt. Within a week's time, he'd witnessed two major miracles. He was in the belly of a great fish and lived to talk about it. And he preached to 120,000 people, and they got saved! You'd think Jonah would be ready to sign up for another assignment from God right then and there! But in fact, he wasn't too thrilled with the miracles. He was so angry that he pouted.

> "But Jonah was greatly displeased and became angry . . . Jonah went out and sat down in a place east of the city. There he made himself a shelter, sat in its shade and waited to see what would happen to the city." (John 4:1,5)

Jonah was upset with God because he wanted the people of Nineveh to suffer God's fierce wrath instead of bathing in His great grace. He didn't like those people one bit, and if you don't like people, you're not a good candidate to be used by God.

By the way, some people are skeptical about the story of Jonah. One time a man asked me, "Pastor do you really believe the book of Jonah?"

I answered with a clarifying question, "What part of it?"

He then said, "The part about that whale swallowing him."

I replied, "If the Bible said that a minnow swallowed him, I'd believe it." Long ago, I'd decided to believe every word of the Bible even if I didn't understand parts of it. After all, God is far bigger than my ability to comprehend Him. He perfectly sees the end from the beginning, but I see only a minute part of reality. He's big enough to give me confidence to trust Him even when I don't see it all—and I never will.

The man was persistent. He prodded, "Come on, Pastor. How do you know it's true?"

I smiled, "Well, I'll ask Jonah when I get to heaven."

He thought for a second, and then he asked, "What if Jonah didn't make it to heaven?"

I looked him square in the eyes and said, "Well, then you can ask him."

Jonah hated the Ninevites. It infuriated him that God actually didn't destroy them. I can picture him sitting under his tree, pouting and saying to God, "I can't believe you saved them, God. They're a no good bunch of people!" In the rest of the story, Jonah argues with God about how He does things.

This is a story of God's grace toward an evil, vicious people, but it's also a story of His patience with one of His servants. Jonah is a lot like many of us. He had an agenda for God, and he expected God to jump through his hoops. It's a sad tale of bitterness, resistance, and unbelief, but we can learn a lot from it. We can examine our hearts to notice the resistance to people who are different from us. We may feel superior or inferior to people of different races, cultures, backgrounds, and bank balances. If we feel superior, we'll despise them and look down on them. If we feel inferior, we'll resent them and hope they fall from the pedestal where we've put them. Both of these perspectives miss the heart of God and prevent us from responding in faith to a God Nudge. God may send a whale along to change our direction, but more often, he lets us wallow in our arrogance or self-pity until we can't stand it any longer. That's a kind of acid, too! Then we'll turn to God for Him to do a work of grace in our hearts—and then He makes us willing instruments in His hands.

Trust God to use you to connect His heart with people He loves.

Are you like Jonah? Has God nudged you to show His love to someone, but you're unwilling because you feel superior or inferior. Get over it! Let the grace of God melt your heart, put steel in your soul, and change your view of every person on the planet. Stop running in the opposite direction. Stop, turn around (or at least wake up when you find yourself on a beach after a great fish spits you out!), and trust God to use you to connect His heart with people He loves. Be willing to take any assignment He gives you—even to love Democrats or Republicans; black, white, yellow or brown skinned people; Baptists, Catholics, and Presbyterians. No one is beyond the grace of God. No one.

Demanding Certainty

Some people resist God Nudges because they insist on God giving them handwriting on the wall, smoke signals, or audible voices. I've sensed God's unmistakable communication many times, but I've never heard an audible voice from Him. A few people simply won't budge without seeing Charlton Heston walk down from a mountain with two rock tablets in his hands. They expect to see a burning bush or a bright light from heaven. They won't respond until a booming voice says, "Hey, you. Yeah, you. It's me, God. Up here. Look at me. I'm talking to you!"

It's probably not going to happen.

God connects with us in many different ways. He often uses the truth of the Bible, and then He applies it with an impression to give us specific direction. We don't hear actual words, but the message is often clear. Isaiah wrote about the voice of God when he penned,

> "Your ears shall hear a word behind you saying this
> is the way, walk in it. Whenever you turn to the right,
> or whenever you turn to the left." (Isaiah 30:21NKJV)

Years ago, I was on my way to San Diego, and I was sitting in the terminal at LAX waiting for my connecting flight. This particular part of the terminal was under construction and the walkways were very narrow. I was reviewing sermon notes on my computer, when a young lady walked in front of me and then sat down a seat away from me. All of a sudden, I felt God telling me to strike up a conversation with her. But I said to myself, *No way! I'm not going to strike up a conversation with this lady. She's going to think I'm trying to flirt with her.* So I dismissed the thought and I continued working on the project on my computer. About five minutes later, my name was called on the loudspeaker: "Mike Robertson, please come to the podium."

I walked up to the desk, and the attendant told me, "Mr. Robertson, we're changing your seat."

"Oh, really," I replied.

"Yes, we're moving you up to first class."

I stammered, "But . . . there must be some mistake. I didn't pay for that."

He smiled, "We need to shift the weight in the plane. We need more weight up front." I must have looked very surprised because he then explained, "Sir, don't worry. It's not going to cost you anything."

I felt relieved. "Well, if it's not going to cost me anything, I'll go to the front any day."

A few minutes later, we boarded the plane. I was still basking in my good fortune of being moved to first-class as I put my bag in the overhead bin and then sat down in seat number four. Guess who was in the seat next to me – that same young lady! I almost laughed as I prayed silently, "Lord, You're playing with me!"

I thought to myself, *Since we're both headed to San Diego I'll just ask her about her favorite restaurant.* I still had some reservations about striking up a conversation with her, so I continued to pray in my head, "Lord, the girl can't be twenty years old. What does she know about restaurants? And besides, she's as skinny as a rail. I bet she doesn't even eat! I know San Diego like the back of my hand. I don't need her advice."

The Lord said again, "Talk to her."

I looked over at the girl next to me and said, "Hey, do you know of any good restaurants in San Diego?"

Her face beamed as she said, "Oh, I sure do!" She began to describe her favorite hamburger joint.

I smiled and nodded, "That's cool." It wasn't exactly a report of five-star restaurants in the city, but I was pretty sure God wasn't interested in hamburgers.

After that, she wouldn't stop talking. She was extremely nervous about flying, and her anxiety spilled out in a torrent of words. She was talking ninety miles an hour. I nodded as she chattered on, but I didn't have any openings to say a word. I began to think, I can shut this down really fast. *I'll just ask her if she knows Jesus. That question stops most conversations.*

When she finally stopped talking long enough to take a breath I said, "Let me interrupt you for a second. I want to ask you a question. Do you know the Lord?"

Her face beamed. "Do I know the Lord?" And she was off again … she began to preach me a sermon … a very long sermon!

Thankfully, it was a short flight. Before we landed, God nudged me again to ask her another question. It wasn't part of the topic of our conversation, but who was I to argue with God at this point? I asked her, "Why aren't you following Christ in the ministry?" She looked stunned. From the look on her face, I could tell this question wasn't out of the blue. She had been wrestling with it for some time. She knew she was supposed to be in the ministry, but she was headed another direction. God used me to talk to her about her resistance.

Earlier in the conversation, she had told me she was moving to Southern California. As our talk was winding down, I asked her if she had decided on a city where she planned to live. She said she was moving to Oceanside, and she asked if I knew of any good churches there. I had planted a church there, so I gave her the church's address and phone number.

As I looked back on that series of promptings, I was initially resistant to the Lord's nudge. I fought it, explained it away, and tried to ignore it. But God was very patient and persistent. He didn't quit on me. Finally, I got the point, and I initiated a wonderful conversation with a young woman I'd never seen in my life. If God Himself had showed up that day in the terminal as we waited for the flight, both of us would have fainted! But God had a different plan, a delivery system to communicate His message: me.

There's a big difference between a good idea and a God idea.

Like the disciples in the gospels, I'm slow to hear, slow to learn, and slow to respond. For that reason, I pray daily that my spiritual ears will be able to hear what the Holy Spirit is speaking to my spirit, that my eyes will be open to see what the Holy Spirit already sees, and that God will give me a heart to discern what God wants me to do. There's a big difference between a good idea and a God idea. I have a lot of good ideas. In fact, I think of them all the time. In addition, I have a lot of burdens about people, causes, and opportunities. But a burden is different than a call. I may be burdened for the people of Somalia, but I'm not called to go minister to the people of Somalia. I'm called to minister to the people in the United States. But when God gives me a burden, I still want to do whatever I can to help those people—in Somalia or anywhere else. If I go about doing all the good ideas that come to mind or I hear about, I'll never get to the God idea for my life.

I also ask God daily to give me courage. This is a crucial part of God Nudges: having the courage to step out in faith and accomplish what God has prompted me to do.

Jesus was called "the Word." It's His nature to communicate with us. The question is: Will we listen and obey. Responding to Him in faith enables us to enjoy the greatest adventure life can offer, and it allows us to avoid a lot of trouble over the years. I've found, too, that my spirit usually picks up on things before my other senses. I may not be sure what the impression means, and I may initially question whether it's from God, but sooner or later, I realize God is nudging me. As the Bible says, "Deep calleth unto deep." I believe the Holy Spirit calls my spirit on a regular basis and leads me in the way I should go. The Christian life isn't just a set of rules or principles. Yes, we believe in propositional truth, but the truth about God tells us that we can have a real relationship with Him. He delights to draw us close. In Paul's most profound letter about spiritual life, he wrote:

> "But if Christ is in you, then even though your body is subject to death because of sin, the Spirit gives life because of righteousness. And if the Spirit of him who raised Jesus from the dead is living in you, he who raised Christ from the dead will also give life to your mortal bodies because of his Spirit who lives in you. . . . For those who are led by the Spirit of God are the children of God."
> (Romans 8:10-11, 14)

I want to have the kind of relationship with God that is so close, so strong, and so intimate that I'm responsive to His leading all day every day.

Mystery of Uncertainty

The Bible contains wonderful promises of a vibrant relationship with God, but it tells the truth about our thick skulls and hard hearts—God's people often resist His nudges. One of the most painful failures described in the Bible occurred after the children of Israel conquered the Promised Land. Life in the Spirit is never easy and smooth. We have to fight every day to know and do God's will. At this point, the people were tired of fighting the Philistines and other armies. They looked around and saw that other nations had powerful kings to lead them. All they had were some priests who wore strange aprons. They didn't realize they already had a king: God Himself. They demanded a new king.

Finally, God gave them what they wanted. Saul, son of Kish, was tall, handsome and rich. He was from one of the best families. He was a sure thing! But things didn't quite work out. God gave Saul a mission to conquer the army and the land of a king named Agag. Saul led his army to victory, but he didn't fulfill God's command to kill Agag and destroy all his property. When Samuel the prophet confronted him, Saul blamed his soldiers! This was just one of the times Saul was disobedient. Eventually, God gave up on him, and directed Samuel to find another king to replace him. It wasn't exactly a smooth transfer of power. Samuel anointed David as the new king, but Saul was still on the throne. Saul tried to kill David many times, chasing him through the desert with his army. Saul's disobedience caused heartache in his own family because his son Jonathan supported his rival, David. Saul's heart became so poisoned by pride and bitterness that demons oppressed him. Not a pretty picture!

Saul hadn't obeyed God's nudges. (In fact, they were more than impressions. They were unmistakable directives from God's priest.) And now he was paying the price. When God replaced him with a new king, Saul wasn't willing to accept God's plan. He attacked David and drove him into the wilderness. But God didn't forget His new king. God led 600 "mighty men" to join David and fight with him. They were misfits in their culture, but they were God's choice men to fight by David's side. He was glad to have them!

At a crucial moment in David's life, God used an unlikely source to nudge him. While David and his men were running from Saul's army, they had to make ends meet any way they could. Some of them earned some money by tending the sheep of a rich man named Nabal. When David's band of men were running out of supplies, he sent some of them to Nabal to ask for help. They explained their need, and they reminded him that they had never stolen anything from him. They had guarded his men and protected his property. David's little army had fought to protect Nabal's land and flocks, but Nabal refused to give them any supplies.

At that point, things began to get ugly. When the men reported Nabal's response to their request, David was furious. He grabbed his sword and led his men back to Nabal's house. The stingy man was going to pay! As they approached Nabal's house, his wife, Abigail, heard they were coming. To stop David's revenge, she rode out to meet him with loads of provisions—the ones Nabal should have given David's men in the first place.

Living on the edge is an uncomfortable but exciting place to be.

David was surprised. She was beautiful and smart, and she stopped David from an act of vengeance. She pleaded with David not to kill her husband—not because Nabal was a noble, good man, but because killing him would tarnish David's reputation and harm his ability to lead when he took the throne.

Abigail, led by a God Nudge, reminded David that he had a divine destiny. He couldn't afford to have the blood of a fool like Nabal on his sword. He needed a clear conscience when he became king. Killing Nabal in a fit of rage would haunt him for a long, long time.

Abigail's courage and grace weren't just a nudge in David's life. They were a shove! He agreed to stop his attack because he recognized the source of her plea. He told her, "God is speaking to me through you."

Abigail could have avoided the risk of warning David before he and his men arrived at her house. She could have let them kill her husband. After all, Nabal's name means, "Fool," and he certainly was one! She responded to the crisis by listening to the Lord, overcoming any resistance of fear, and taking bold action. And David listened to her. He realized God was using her to nudge him, so he changed direction.

I'm amazed at Abigail's faith and courage. How did she overcome her fear of meeting this outlaw named David? King Saul was trying to kill him. Wasn't he dangerous? How did she know the right thing to do? I think it's very simple: her spirit sensed God's leading. How did she know her efforts were going to be successful? She didn't. In fact, she took a huge risk. She just stepped out in faith when she sensed a God Nudge. I'm sure she was nervous. (I'm always nervous when I sense God nudging me.) She realized that if God didn't give her favor in David's eyes, his first victim could have been her! If God didn't show up, she would be in big trouble.

That's the inherent nature of a God Nudge. We respond in faith, but we never know where it will lead. Sometimes people respond positively to our message, but sometimes they think we're nuts—or worse. Living on the edge is an uncomfortable but exciting place to be. I like the thrill of it. I know I'm pleasing

God when I'm trying to walk by faith. The Bible says,

> "Without faith it is impossible to please God, because anyone who comes to Him must believe that He exists and that He rewards those who earnestly seek Him." (Hebrews 11:6 NKJV)

Living by faith always involves risk, and many times, there's a cost. Every person who walks with God lives with a blend of mystery and certainty. We never know where and how God will lead us, but we're supremely confident in His wisdom, love, and power to accomplish His purposes.

Don't wait for all the conditions to be just right. Abigail didn't wait until she knew everything was going to work out perfectly. As a matter of fact, she realized her efforts could prove disastrous if David didn't believe her message was from God. Yet, she stepped out, saved her family, and protected the reputation of her next king. She probably fought a host of intense emotions as she led those donkeys up the hill to meet David and his men, but she kept taking steps forward. When emotions rule our lives, our courage weakens. But when we put ourselves in God's hands and respond in faith, we can keep moving forward even when our emotions scream for us to stop.

Needing Immediate Confirmations

Sometimes when I respond to a God Nudge, I tell people things that may not quite fit their situations at the present. If they don't apply right now, they'll need to remember them for later reference. God wants people to be prepared to respond in faith when the time is right. Jesus told His disciples countless times that He was going to Jerusalem to be tried, tortured, and killed to pay for mankind's sins. He wanted them to be ready when it happened. (All but John somehow missed the message and ran like schoolgirls when he was arrested, but that's a different story.)

Over the years, I've told a lot of people words from God that weren't immediately applicable. I sensed God wanted to warn them, encourage them, or get them to start gathering resources for the future. Sometimes, people look at me like I've lost my mind. I may tell them God wants them to get married, go into ministry, start a business, or something else. Some of these people have already been thinking of it, but for many, it has never crossed their minds. When I give them a word and it doesn't make sense to them, I feel very uncomfortable, but I'm only the messenger. It's up to God to give them faith to respond to His nudge.

Guilty Conscience

One of the biggest factors in causing resistance is unresolved, unforgiven guilt. I've been a pastor for a long time, and I've observed that many people beat themselves up on a daily basis. When they fail, they call themselves horrible names. They feel they aren't worthy of God's forgiveness and love, so they give up on God or try to do some act of penance to make up for their sins. Guilt crushes their spirits. God uses our consciences to steer us away from sin and toward Him. His goal is never to blast us. When He convicts us of sin, He wants to remind us of His wonderful forgiveness, love, and acceptance. Jesus took the punishment we deserve so we can receive His love and kindness. We don't need to punish ourselves any longer!

It's my job to be a mouthpiece of grace, to help people believe in themselves again, and encourage them to believe in God again. God is more than willing to point out their sin. I'm not the sin police. I'm not like the prophets in the Old Testament who were sent to tell people everything they were doing wrong. That's not my job. Holy Spirit's role is to convict people of sin, but when He does, He reminds them of His forgiveness. When I talk to people I'm not dealing with their sinful side, I'm dealing with the potential side of their life—that great things are about to happen!

Self Doubt

A few years ago, I was speaking at a growing church in Steamboat Springs, Colorado. I had prepared the sermon, but as I got into the service, God began to give me indications of things going on in people's lives. Usually when I'm in a service, I deal with the blessed side of life. I don't harp on negative things and condemn people. It's not my job to call people out and embarrass them. When God nudges me in the middle of a worship service, I let the audience know, "Don't be afraid. As a matter of fact, have faith and maybe God will say something to you today. Don't be afraid that I'm going to deal with the negative side of your life."

Be faithful and obedient to God, and leave the results to Him.

When it came time for me to speak during the service, I put the sermon aside and gave everybody encouraging words from heaven. When I walked away, however, I had second thoughts. I wondered if I'd done the right thing by ditching my prepared sermon to share God nudges with the people. Self-doubt and guilt began to plague me.

A couple of years later, I ran into the pastor and his staff at a convention. I told the pastor, "I guess my message at your church was a bomb since you never invited me back to speak."

He looked surprised and reassured me, "Oh, no. Quite the contrary."

He turned and introduced me to a lady. She explained, "You told my husband, 'You need to get busy for God.' Those few words turned his life around. For years, he had been on the sidelines. He was following God from a distance, but now he's serving as an elder in our church."

If you don't get immediate confirmation that a God Nudge was right on target, don't be alarmed, and don't beat yourself up. Be faithful and obedient to God, and leave the results to Him. But I'm not naïve. I'm well aware that I'm a flawed vessel, or as Paul describes us, "a cracked pot"! After I've spoken a word God has given me for someone, I often pray,

> "Lord, that which is of your Holy Spirit, let it prosper. That which was not of your Holy Spirit and was just a good idea that I had in my spirit, please don't let those things prosper. And don't let anything of my flesh prosper. Don't let that seed find any root. Just have the people brush it off."

AWOL Saints

Sometimes, I have a God Nudge for somebody during a church service, but during the service they've slipped out. I almost always wait until after the message to share those words with people, but sometimes, people are AWOL: absent without leave. When that happens, I wonder: Was it a real God Nudge? Maybe I was mistaken and God was protecting them from my errant statement, or maybe impure motives were prompting me to say something I shouldn't say. It can happen. I deeply desire for God to bless people, but sometimes I can get ahead of God.

I need to be careful about that. Most of the time, though, I'm confident when I give someone a word from the Lord. I've had plenty of practice, and God has given me a sensitive spirit to notice my motives.

But there might be another reason a person has left the building when it's time for me to share a nudge: The person may sense the Spirit has something to say, but does not want to hear it. People can abort a God Nudge from getting to them simply by walking out of a service. When I've seen someone walk out, I have asked the ushers to try and go find the person. Sometimes they find him or her, and sometimes they don't. Some of the richest conversations happen when people find the courage to walk back in and talk with me. The process of running and returning softens their hearts and makes them pliable in God's hands. It's a beautiful thing to see.

In our church, people have learned to expect God to give plenty of nudges. They may have been surprised in the past, but not any longer. Many people come with expectant hearts. They pray, "God, are you going to speak to me today?" "Lord, do you want to do something through me today?" One person who believes God is formidable, but a group of people is a powerhouse! Jesus said, "Where two or more are gathered together in My name, there I am in the midst of them" (Matthew 18:20). Expectant, faithful, encouraging people are fertile soil for God to produce incredible growth. They are logs on a fire ready to ignite. I love being with people like this! The miraculous takes place when we get together as groups of faith-filled people. That's the place where God delights in nudging us.

Fear And Faith – Strange Bed Fellows

Some people believe words from God come with no worries or

fears. On the contrary. If you're going to be used by God, you will have realize that fear and faith often exist together. Fear is like a warning light on the dashboard of an automobile: It causes us to pay attention. Fear is normal. Statistics tell us that more auto accidents occur close to our homes than far away. Why is that? It's because we are so familiar with our surroundings that we often get careless. When I'm in an unfamiliar city, I'm much more cautious and obedient to road signs. I don't take rolling stops away from my city's streets. The same principle applies when we step out in faith. We're not in our comfort zone, so fear is quite normal.

For a time, I served as Vice President of Advancement for Southwestern Assemblies of God University in Waxahachie, Texas. We had a regular chapel service. One afternoon, the President of the college stopped by my office and asked if I would preach in chapel the next day. I told him that if I could spend the afternoon with the Lord, I'd be happy to speak in chapel. I went home to be alone, and I asked the Lord what he would have me say to these young people.

As I was praying, an unusual experience happened. I saw a vision of a young lady. I was sure she was going to show up in that chapel the next day. I could see her face very clearly, and in fact, I could see the blouse she was wearing. The name that came to mind was Brittney.

The next morning in chapel service about a thousand students and faculty filed into the auditorium. I preached the message, but before I finished, I told them I wanted all the Brittneys to come to the front of the chapel at the conclusion of the service. I knew that was very strange. I'd never said anything like that before. I explained, "If your first name is Brittney, come to the front. The Lord told me to help one of you."

At the end of the service, we dismissed the crowd. Soon, about fifteen young ladies walked up to the front. I looked carefully at each one of them, but none of them fit the image of the girl in the vision that I had seen the day before. Fear began to settle in me like never before. I was praying, "Lord, none of these girls looks like her. What do I do now?" I began to go down the line and tell the girls, "I'm sorry, it's not you. No, it's not you. Thank you for coming, but it's not you." I was sure because the girl in the vision had a dark complexion, but most of these girls were Caucasian.

I got to the end of the line of Brittneys, and I was very discouraged. At that moment, the girl that I saw in the vision—the exact face, the exact blouse—stepped up to talk to her friend, whose name was Brittney. As soon as I saw her, the Lord said, "Give her $500 for her school bill."

I walked over to her and asked, "Is your name Brittney?"

She replied, "No."

It finally sank in. The face and the name were two different pieces of the puzzle. I asked, "So . . . is that your friend, Brittney?"

"Yes," she replied, but she was very curious about the line of this conversation.

Fear is not a signal to turn back; it's a sign to go forward and exercise faith

I asked a few questions, and she told me she had come from a foreign country to study to be a youth pastor. She was excited about what she was learning, but she had a problem: She wasn't able to pay her expenses. If she didn't find some money in a few days, she was going to have to go home. I told her the Lord was prompting me to give her $500. She was blown away. So was I. The God Nudge kept her in college and prepared her for a lifetime of effective ministry.

Fear is not a signal to turn back; it's a sign to go forward and exercise faith. Fear and other negative emotions often rear their heads when we're involved in the work of God. If we wait for them to go away, we'll miss out on countless opportunities to be used by God. We need to recognize our fears, but then move past them and rely on God like never before. Virtually every great story in the Bible is about overcoming some form of fear. When we notify heaven that we're candidates to be used by God, we need to be prepared for some very unusual things to occur. Are you ready for some things that are out of the normal? Faith and fear go hand in hand.

Living On the Edge

There was a t-shirt I saw many years ago that read: *If you're not living on the edge, you're taking up too much space.* I'm not advocating foolish risks. That's dumb. But walking with the mysterious, infinite God always involves adventure. It's part of the abundant life Christ promised to those who know Him and follow Him.

God want us to "put on a heart of compassion, kindness, humility, gentleness, and patience" (Colossians 3:12), but occasionally, He wants us to be as bold as a lion. Many years ago, soon after I trusted Christ as my Savior, I was sitting in church before the service started. I was a bus captain in the church, but this week, I was off-duty. One of the other bus drivers came to me and asked, "My niece is here from another state. She doesn't know anybody. Would you mind being her friend and sitting with her? I'd like to, but I've have to drive the bus."

Of course I was glad to help, so he introduced me to his niece, and we sat near the back row in the service. A group of teenagers sat down behind us. They were very talkative, very disruptive, and it was extremely annoying.

I didn't know if the young lady with me was born again, and

I wasn't even sure if she was interested in God. The kids behind us were causing such a problem that we couldn't enjoy the singing or hear the pastor's message. I began to get angry—not at the inconvenience to me, but that these kids were preventing my friend's niece from hearing from God. I didn't know how to respond to the situation, but God gave me a clear nudge. The Lord gave me this word to share with them: "If this young lady beside me doesn't give her heart to Jesus Christ, her blood will be on your shoulders."

I didn't want to say this harsh word to the kids. I was afraid they'd laugh at me, or worse, that my friend's niece would think I was nuts. To keep from making a scene, I wrote it down on a scrap of paper in my Bible. Near the end of the service, I turned around and handed the piece of paper to the group of young people, and I headed down to the altar. I told the young lady I was going down to the front to pray. I knelt and asked the Lord to work powerfully in the hearts of these disruptive kids. I think I also prayed they wouldn't jump me after the service! I also asked God to work in the young lady's heart. After the service, everybody went home. It was pretty anticlimactic.

About a year passed, and I forgot about the day we sat in front of the unruly teenagers. One day as I walked down the hall of the Bible College, a young lady came up to me. She asked, "Do you remember me?" She could tell I couldn't remember her, so she continued, "I'm the girl that sat with you in church last year."

"Oh, yes," I remarked. "Sure, I remember you. How are you doing?"

She was filled with joy and explained, "I've just enrolled in the Bible College."

I asked, "That's great! So . . . you've given your heart to the Lord?"

"Oh, yes," she said, "I've wanted to tell you that I saw such dedication in your life that day, so I gave my heart to Jesus Christ."

We have many forms of resistance to God Nudges. Denying our skepticism and fear doesn't help us overcome them and respond in faith. Instead, we need to be honest about our resistance, talk to God about it, and trust Him to give us courage to respond in faith. God is looking for agents of change. It's one of the most challenging and thrilling roles we'll ever play. Don't let fear, guilt, or confusion keep you on the sidelines.

Think about it...

1. How does pride—superiority or inferiority— poison our hearts and keep us from hearing God's loving voice?

2. We don't want to be foolish and jump to conclusions, but at what point does demanding certainty keep us on the sidelines instead of responding in faith to God Nudges?

3. How can we overcome our normal fears when we sense God nudging us?

4. What are some ways guilt crushes our spirits?

5. As you consider these forms of resistance, what are some steps of progress you'd like to take?

Chapter 6

Risk-Takers

God Nudges always require us to face risks. I love nature, and as I've watched animals, I've noticed something very significant: A turtle only makes progress when he sticks out his neck. In the same way, unless we're willing to take action in response to God Nudges, we won't make any progress.

Karen and I have always been risk-takers. It's a part of our lives. Our decision to get married—as every married person knows—was taking a risk (more for her than for me, but that's a different story). If you invest in the stock market, you're taking a risk. If you drive a car, especially in Southern California, you're taking your life in your hands. Even becoming a Christian is a risk because you don't know where God will lead you. When you gave ten percent of your money to God for the first time, you were taking a major risk. We take risks every day in every part of our lives, but we need to be wise about our risk-taking.

Abraham's Nudge

Genesis has an account of a man many people don't recognize. His name is Terah. Unless you really enjoy digging into the linage of people in the Bible, reading Genesis 11 can be a little boring. We find name after name and begat after begat. There are people listed we've never read about before and will never hear from again, but near the end of the chapter, we read:

> "Terah took his son Abram, his grandson Lot son of Haran, and his daughter-in-law Sarai, the wife

> of his son Abram, and together they set out from Ur of the Chaldeans to go to Canaan. But when they came to Haran, they settled there." (Genesis 11:31)

Terah received a call to go to Canaan, but he settled in Haran. We don't know why he stopped before he got to the place God told him to go. He may have been tired, or maybe his kids spilled French fries in the back of the van and he got mad at them. He just couldn't keep going! But Terah didn't go to Canaan. He may have felt more comfortable in Haran. Maybe he heard there were giants in the land of Canaan. Certainly, others gave that report many years later. Terah worshipped the moon god, so he may have found other moon god worshippers in Haran, and he liked it better there. We can ask a lot of questions, but the Bible doesn't provide any answers about Terah's choice. However, one thing is certain: Terah ended his journey short of where God wanted him to go. He settled for something less than what God wanted to give him. He wasn't willing to take a risk and follow through completely with God's leading.

For years, Terah's family stayed in Haran, but when he died, Abram (later called Abraham) received another nudge from God:

> "Go from your country, your people and your father's household to the land I will show you. I will make you into a great nation, and I will bless you, I will make your name great and you will be a blessing." (Genesis 12:1)

When Abraham lived in the Ur of the Chaldeans, he was "living large and in charge." Modern excavations of Chaldean ruins unearthed an affluent part of town where they believe Abraham lived. Two-story buildings weren't common in ancient cultures, but they were discovered in this city. When Ur of Chaldeans was dug up in 1922, archeologists found tablets with trigonometry problems on them that still haven't been solved. (Talk about tough homework!)

In this affluent community and advanced culture, Abraham heard a God Nudge: "Get up, leave your family, and go." His father, Terah, had gotten that word from God, but he stopped in Haran. If Terah had completed the journey, we might list him as one of the patriarchs of the faith. Instead of "the God of Abraham, Isaac, and Jacob," we might read "the God of Terah, Abraham, Isaac, and Jacob." We'll never know what caused Terah to stay, but we know that Abraham responded to God's nudge and went to Canaan.

In the list of faith's heroes in the book of Hebrews, we read, "Abraham heard the Lord, and he did not trouble his mind about where he was going." (Hebrews 11:8 Amplified Bible) Why did he take action and step out in faith? Because he heard from God and was willing to take a risk to obey Him.

God Nudges always involve risk.

God Nudges always involve risk. When we sense God's prompting, we may feel a surge of fear, but it's exhilarating, too. When we respond in faith, God gives us a burst of energy to leave the security of the present for the uncertainty of the future. When we step out, we renounce the comfortable and embrace the possible.

Sometimes, however, we don't get the God Nudge quite right. We think of Abraham as one of the noblest men of our faith, but he didn't get it completely right even when he responded to God. If you look closely at the story in Genesis, you'll see that he was told to leave his family behind—but he didn't. He took Lot with him when he left Haran. The Lord had told Abraham to leave his family members. Sometimes we get in trouble because we want to take everybody with us.

When I was starting out in ministry and saw the blessing of the Lord, I envisioned a day when all of my friends and I would enjoy a faith journey together. Since then, I've learned that many of our childhood friends won't join us. We can invite them, but if they choose not to go, we shouldn't hang back with them and miss the adventure God has for us. Abraham took Lot, and it was a big mistake. Lot soon became a thorn in Abraham's side. If you keep reading the narrative in Genesis, Abraham repeatedly had to rescue Lot from all kinds of calamities. When they came to a point of sharp disagreement, Abraham told Lot to choose which piece of land he wanted, and of course, Lot chose the best part. Later, Abraham had to rescue Lot out of sin-infested Sodom and Gomorrah. The nagging and complex problems between Lot and Abraham could have been averted if Abraham had listened more carefully to the God Nudge. Abraham's sin of being nice cost him immensely. May God deliver us from the "sin of niceness". Still, the pattern of his life was to continually pursue God, responding to God's promises and trusting Him to provide.

Types of Risk Takers

Are you willing to take risks for God? Risky faith isn't easy or safe. It challenges us to the core. If it were easy, everyone would be doing it. If the risk is scary, we open a door for a miracle. There's nothing like stepping out in faith with no safety net, trusting God to do what only He can do. When you experience the thrill of seeing God work this extraordinary way, you never want go back to an ordinary life.

The size of the risk determines the size of your reward. Different people, though, have different perceptions and responses to risk. Let's look at three types of people.

1. Undertakers

Some people live in the past. About ten percent of us focus on "the good old days". However, when our memories become bigger than our dreams, we're in trouble. Memories can be helpful because they remind us what God has done. With faith-filled hindsight, our memories can stimulate us to trust Him even more today. But some people don't make this connection. They live in the past without using it as a springboard to trust God for greater things today.

I don't dwell that much on memories, I spend most of my time dreaming, trusting God to stimulate my faith, and taking risks. Our dreams for the future have to be bigger than our memories of the past. When we live in the past, we strangle our faith and choke the life out of our walks with God. Gradually, we live like we're already dead. We're ready for the undertaker instead of being an overcomer.

2. Caretakers

Many people, perhaps forty percent of believers, are in maintenance mode. They're preoccupied with what needs to happen right now with their kids, their homes, their businesses, their health, and every other aspect of life. They don't spend much time, if any, dreaming about the possibilities of the future. These people manage most families and organizations, and they do a good job making things work. They think often and deeply about meeting today's needs. They plan and organize resources to meet the demands of the moment. Their goal is to minimize risk at all costs. They run calculations every minute of every day to be sure they feel completely safe and secure. Living on the edge? That's not their goal at all. When they read the Bible, they seem to miss the fact that Jesus often talked about the future: His death, resurrection, and future glory. All they see in the Scriptures are management principles to apply today.

3. Risk-Takers

Every leader, every entrepreneur, every inventor, every church planter, and every person who makes a big difference in the lives of others is a risk-taker. Some are wild and crazy, and some are more calculated, but about half of the population is in this category. America has become a great nation and the church is reaching millions because these people are willing to lay it all on the line.

Risk-takers squeeze all they can out of today so they can be all God wants them to be tomorrow. They have the capacity to face both success and failure. In fact, they learn to be comfortable with failure. Instead of being defensive and angry, they learn from their setbacks. They apply hard won lessons to their next steps forward. To them, failure is the backdoor to success. Theodore Roosevelt remarked, "No one is worth their salt who is not ready at all times to risk their well being, to risk their body and to risk their life for a better cause."[4]

What type of person are you: undertaker, caretaker, or risk-taker? Do you live in the past or the present, or do you have a sense that God has a glorious future waiting for you? Reflect on your thoughts, prayers, and conversations over the past week.

---

[4]Cited in Inspirational Writings of Elbert Hubbard (Kessinger Publishing, 2005), 137.

How many of them focused on pleasant memories and painful "should have beens"? How many were concerns about the day's events and relationships? How many were dreams and plans to see God do wonderful things in the future? No one is a pure dreamer. Even visionaries have to reflect on the past and make choices about the present, but they keep their eye on the glorious future God has for them.

I often ask myself, am I doing anything that is big enough to attract God's attention? Am I willing to lay everything on the line for a God Nudge? And how about you? When was the last time you colored outside the lines? When was the last time that you took a risk of faith?

Many of us try to avoid risks at all costs. Of course, risk doesn't have value in itself. It's the object of the risk that has value—or not. And there are many different factors that determine if the risk is worth taking. But if our answer is always "No," or "Wait," or "You've got to be kidding!" we need to reassess our risk tolerance. Does everything have to be a guaranteed success? Is failure too much of a threat? Can you handle every situation without God's intervention and resources? That's not the way I want to live.

I'm willing to accept the possibility of failure because I know that taking risks is the only way to see God do incredible things. There are no guarantees. Sometimes, I've fallen flat on my face, but I'm convinced God is far more pleased with me being willing to take a risk than always playing it safe. And there are, in fact, guarantees. God promises to use every circumstance, even our failures, for good if we'll trust Him (Romans 8:28). I can live with that, and in fact, I can take risks based on His promise.

Is There a Word?

Aside from David, Jehoshaphat was perhaps the best king God's people ever had. As the king of Judah, he restored the spiritual life of the nation. He was a great man and a really good king. When the nations around him went to war, they wanted Jehoshaphat to go with them because they knew the favor of God was upon him. At one point, Jehoshaphat agreed to go into battle with the evil king of Israel. He was the son of King Ahab and Queen Jezebel, who were the two most despicable leaders in Israel's history. The prophet Elijah had fought the wickedness of Ahab. He prophesized that Jezebel would die from a fall from a window, and dogs would eat her flesh. It happened just as Elijah predicted.

By the time Jehoshaphat was king, however, Elijah had died and passed his mantel of leadership and power to Elisha. He listened to the voice of the Lord, understood the mind of God, and was radical in his obedience. That's a key ingredient in responding to God Nudges: radical obedience.

A war was on the near horizon. The kings of Edom, Israel and Judah were ready for battle. These nations hated each other, but they joined forces to fight the King of Moab. For protection, they insisted that Elisha go with them. In difficult times, righteous people often are swept up with the unrighteous. Elisha found himself in a very difficult situation. The three kings and their allied armies ran out of water. A person can live for many days without food, but a much shorter time without water. And marching armies can't last long at all without it. Someone had miscalculated, and the armies were without water for seven long days in the desert.

> *God wants to give us a word for every situation we face.*

As the predicament deepened, Jehoshaphat pleaded, "Is there no longer a prophet of the Lord here whom we can inquire of?" (2 Chronicles 18:6)

Someone finally realized Elisha was there. "He used to pour water on the hands of Elijah," one of the king's advisors said. "Jehoshaphat said Elisha can hear from God for us. Let's go down there and visit with him."

Elisha saw them coming, and he was conflicted in his soul. He had respected Jehoshaphat, but the king was in an alliance with the idol worshipper from Edom, and the son of Ahab and Jezebel, Jahorum, the King of Israel. When they asked Elisha to give them a word from God, he ignored them. Finally, he told them, "Had it not been for the King of Judah, Jehoshaphat, we wouldn't even go to God for the two of you." If it hadn't been for Jehoshaphat, Elisha would have let them die of thirst. The prophet was willing to help because one man had been faithful to God.

Elisha said, "Bring me a musical instrument." They began to play the musical instrument, and Elisha received a God Nudge. He instructed, "Dig this valley full of ditches." That was a harsh word. The men were exhausted and weak from thirst. But Elisha told them, "Dig this valley full of ditches for thus says the Lord. He will bring a great deliverance. We will have water tomorrow."

Elisha's words came true the next day. God filled the ditches with water, and three armies were saved. They defeated the army of Moab in battle. It was a glorious day for Elisha and the three kings.

We learn a valuable lesson from this event: When our backs are against the wall, and when we're in a difficult situation, we need to ask the same question Jehoshaphat asked: "Is there not a word from the Lord?"

God wants to give a word for every situation we face. When the people of God pray and listen for a word, He is ready, willing, and able to speak from heaven. He delivered His word through a man committed to radical obedience. He could have used an angel, but they would have been terrified by the sight. He could have used a flood, but it would have killed them all. Instead, he chose a person "whose heart was completely His": Elisha. God is looking for people like Elisha today.

RISKS AND RESPONSIVENESS

It's thrilling to sense God's prompting and see Him work miracles when we respond to Him, but we need to remember that we're junior partners in the arrangement. We see only a little of what God is doing. He knows the end from the beginning, and many things don't make sense to us. When we think we've got a handle on God, we'd better think again! Humility is another essential ingredient in responding to God. Risk takers may be bold, but they need to develop a healthy sense of God's greatness and their littleness. When we listen to God and sense His leading, we're on the edge of a great mystery.

Jesus told the apostles to be witnesses in Jerusalem, Judea, Samaria, and the rest of the world. The church in Jerusalem soon grew so big and so fast that the apostles had to find some people to help them meet all the needs of the crowds. They appointed seven men who were faithful and faith-filled as deacons. One of them, a man named Philip, went beyond his job description. He shared the gospel with all kinds of people, including those the Jewish people traditionally despised—the Samaritans.

In Samaria, Phillip had held a tremendous revival: the fireworks of God were popping! People were getting born again, healed, and filled with the Holy Spirit. Seemingly out of nowhere, God told him, "I want you to get out of this town and go down to an isolated road in the desert." It was an odd nudge because God was doing great things through him in Samaria. Why send him somewhere else?

As a pastor, I can imagine the questions swirling in Philip's head. *Why leave now? Why an isolated road in the middle of the desert? Is this really You, God?* Philip's faith was severely tested. God was asking him to leave a red hot, fiery service to hang out on a dusty dirt road! Most of us couldn't do it—or more accurately, many of us simply wouldn't do it.

But Philip was devoted to radical obedience. He didn't live for success, and he didn't live for applause. He lived to please an "Audience of One." Whatever his misgivings may have been, he left the city and went to the desert road. There, he waited. After a while, a man came by in a chariot. He was an official in the queen's court of Ethiopia. He was a eunuch who had tried to worship God at the temple in Jerusalem, but of course, they didn't let him in. He wasn't Jewish, he was a foreigner, and he was a eunuch. He may have been discouraged by the rejection, but he was still pursuing God.

As the chariot approached, Philip realized the eunuch was reading a passage in Isaiah—a prophecy about the Messiah who would come. When Philip approached the official, the man explained that he didn't understand what he was reading. Philip explained to him that the passage was talking about Jesus. The official was convinced by Philip's message. He trusted in Jesus, and they stopped the chariot to baptize him. The eunuch was born again and baptized in water in one day! He had gone to the center of Jewish faith and culture, but had been turned away. Then, on a lonely, deserted desert road, God sent someone to tell him the good news about Jesus. The eunuch then went back and introduced the message of Jesus to the officials of Ethiopia, as he was the nation's treasurer. Philip went from speaking to a few hundred people to infecting a whole nation.

God wasn't finished with Philip. As soon as he baptized the eunuch,

> "... the Spirit of the Lord suddenly took Philip
> away. . . . Philip, however, appeared in Azotus
> and traveled about, preaching the gospel in all
> the towns until he reached Caesarea." (Acts 8:39-40)

How did he get from the pool in the desert to the town of Azotus? We don't know. Maybe he walked, or maybe God transported him compliments of Holy Spirit Airlines. However he got there, he kept taking risks to tell people about Jesus. Steven had already been stoned for his faith, so Philip must have known that in every city and town he could possibly face the same fate. However, nothing would stop him from obeying the prompting of God.

Note that Philip's first line on his job description was to serve as a deacon. He wasn't a super-apostle, and he wasn't one of the original twelve disciples, but he was so committed to God that he didn't wait for someone else to take a bold risk to tell people about Jesus. In the same way, every believer is called to radical obedience. There aren't super-Christians and ordinary-Christians. We're all crucial to God's plan to redeem people around the world. We all play important parts in God's design. Earlier, we looked at Peter's description of our common role as believers. It fits again here. He wrote about our identity, our role, and our passion:

> "But you are a chosen people, a royal priesthood,
> a holy nation, God's special possession, that you
> may declare the praises of Him who called you
> out of darkness into His wonderful light." (1 Peter 2:9)

Give yourself to radical obedience, and you will become one of heaven's choicest go-to people to help others find and follow Jesus Christ.

A Compassionate Heart

In his life and ministry, Philip overcame some of the "devil's tricks." Pride has caused many great men and women of God to fall. When God uses us greatly, we need to be very careful not to become full of ourselves. We hear Satan whisper, "Wow, you're pretty sharp! God really needs you to accomplish His will and touch people's lives." No, He doesn't. He can accomplish His purposes with or without us. Being used by God isn't a right; it's the greatest privilege we can experience, and we need to remember that it's a gift of His grace. If evil can't stop you with a blatant sin, Satan will try to get you to fall through pride. I have a suspicion Philip patterned his heart and his ministry after Jesus. Jesus lived to give, not to get. He came to give His life as a ransom for many, not to win accolades or acquire power. Paul reminds us to focus on the love, forgiveness, and grace of Jesus as our model and motivation:

Being used by God isn't a right; it's the greatest privilege we can experience.

> "Therefore if you have any encouragement from being united with Christ, if any comfort from His love, if any common sharing in the Spirit, if any tenderness and compassion, then make my joy complete by being like-minded, having the same

> love, being one in spirit and of one mind. Do nothing out of selfish ambition or vain conceit. Rather, in humility value others above yourselves, not looking to your own interests but each of you to the interests of the others." (Philippians 2:1-4)

How pure and deep was Jesus' motivation to give His life for others—with no strings attached? Matthew tells us that He was watching the crowd one day, much like standing in a stairwell at a college university or high school campus, and He was "moved with compassion" (Matthew 9:36). The Greek word isn't a shallow, weak concept. It means that Jesus was powerfully and deeply moved. He felt their pain and cared about their predicament. The term actually says Jesus was moved "in His bowel." It's the gut-wrenching feeling we get when we've lost a loved one or care deeply because someone we love is in trouble.

If responding to God's prompting is only a game to you, then you're not ready for a God Nudge. If you think it will impress people, then you should fall on your knees and repent of your arrogance. But if your heart is broken for those in need, you're ready to be God's partner in delivering His messages of love and hope.

In the same passage, Jesus instructed His disciples to pray that more workers will join them in the harvest. He said,

> "The harvest is plentiful but the workers are few. Ask the Lord of the harvest to send forth workers." (Matthew 9:37)

Who are the people who are answers to these prayers? Certainly the ones who gathered in the upper room at Pentecost, the thousands who came to Christ in the towns around Jerusalem, and the millions in the Roman world who responded to the gospel in the first three or four centuries after Christ was raised from the tomb. But you and I are also answers to this prayer. We're workers in the vast harvest field, and we have the incredible honor of working side by side with others who are radically obedient to God. Jesus and the disciples prayed that you and I would show up, respond to God Nudges, and be intrinsically motivated to extend His love to hurting people.

EVERY BELIEVER, EVERY DAY

If we depend on paid pastors and church workers to fulfill God's purposes to care for every person in every community throughout the world, the job won't get done. There will be a few exhausted workers and a bunch who are bored. That's not the way the kingdom of God is supposed to operate! In our church, countless people give their hearts, time, and talents to park cars, usher, set up rooms, and do all the other things that have to be done. The reason they're involved, though, isn't just to be busy. They're committed to do their part to reach the lost, care for the hurting, and build believers in their faith. They are the backbone of our fellowship. To be the people God wants us to be, we need the radical obedience of Philip, the compassion of Jesus, and an unbroken focus on His purposes. We encounter countless distractions. Most of them look innocent and attractive, but if we lose our laser focus, we'll settle for the good instead of the great. Don't let that happen to you. Rivet your heart on Jesus, and find a few people who are totally sold out to Him. Encourage each other to love God with all your hearts and take bold steps of faith.

Think about it…

1. Which type of risk taker are you? What would help you to be bold and take more risks?

2. What are some ways pride can appear when we've seen God use us? How can we develop true humility?

3. How would you define and describe "radical obedience"?

4. Who is the most compassionate, bold person you know? Is that person's life attractive to you? Why or why not? What can you learn from this person?

5. What is the most important lesson you've learned from this chapter? How will you make it part of your life?

Chapter 7

Nudges and Money

The way we handle money is a good indication of the condition of our hearts. Jesus had a lot to say about it, and in my experience, a significant percentage of God Nudges relate to finances. Money is far more than pieces of paper and chunks of metal. For many people, it promises to provide the things they desperately want. For others, it's a way to honor God.

Types of People

If we look closely at how people handle money, we'll notice several different motivations and practices.

Some people use money to give them power over others. They give to gain leverage over employees or family members; or they withhold money for the same reason. To them, life is about being one-up in every relationship. Money is simply a tool—a very effective tool—to wield their power. We may think of business executives as those who use money this way, but anyone, rich or poor, can give or hold back money to manipulate others to get what they want. To them, money is all about controlling others.

I've known plenty of people who use money to win approval. They buy the best cars and the finest clothes. They take friends to the best restaurants and enjoy lavish vacations. It's all designed to impress anyone who's watching. Many of the commercials on television are designed to promote this motivation. We simply can't be happy, they tell us, unless we have the latest (and most expensive) stuff to make our friends say, "Wow!"

Other people spend their money for another purpose: to be

as comfortable as possible. They don't care much about impressing anyone. Instead, they're devoted to pleasure, excitement, and protecting themselves from any hassles. They buy nice furniture and the best electronics, and they enjoy an extravagant lifestyle. How can we tell they're devoted to comfort? When something doesn't work as well as they expected, or a waiter at a fine restaurant is a little slow, or their vacation isn't all they hoped, they get mad!

Some people use money in the opposite way. They long for security, so they save every penny. They clip coupons, look for deals, and often check their bank balance. They worry they won't have enough to pay their bills, even when they have far more money than they really need.

How do these types of people relate to a God Nudge? It's pretty easy to imagine. They're preoccupied with something other than God and His kingdom, so they aren't very open to God Nudging them to give generously, cheerfully, and creatively to help others. As we've seen, the primary trait of someone who is responsive to God is a heart filled with His love, forgiveness, and strength. When we feel secure and loved by God, we don't feel compelled to use money for selfish purposes—as a tool of power, to impress people, to lavish ourselves with comfort and excitement, or to hoard it so we'll feel safe.

A friend told me a story about a woman who has a sensitive spirit. She loves to give to others, and God often nudges her to be generous—not just to write checks for needy people, but to give her time and possessions, too. In fact, she sometimes senses that God wants her to give away something she really values. She's given away a painting, a fine table, a piece of heirloom jewelry, and other things that have been important to her. Her husband, by the way, sometimes thinks she's nuts, but he's learned to avoid getting in the way of God's obvious nudges in her life. Every time she gives something she values, she thinks and prays about it. She reflects on the truth that Jesus gave her everything; so giving away something of value puts her close to His heart. She remarked, "I love giving these things. I try to give them to people who really need them, and it gives me great pleasure to see the looks on their faces." Sometimes, though, she gives anonymously. She actually gets even more delight from giving without anyone knowing the source.

THE JOY OF GIVING

God Nudges about money can come at any time. I often find that when I'm able to get away from the daily pressures, I'm more conscious of God's leading. It's been my practice to get away for at least a day every few weeks to pray, study and listen for the ever-present voice of God. On one of these days away from the rat race, I was out for a morning walk. When I crossed the street in front of a hotel, I noticed a couple of men who had obviously slept in their car in the parking lot. How did I know? Their socks were hanging out the window. I felt a God Nudge to ask them if they needed any help, but I ignored it and continued to walk down the road.

When I came back on my walking loop, they were still there. I knew God was giving me another opportunity to respond to His nudge, so I stopped. I tapped on the window and said, "Hey, I was wondering if you need some help."

The two young men looked a little embarrassed, and one of them said, "No, we're fine."

I was about to walk away, but then I got an even stronger impression to give them a $100 bill. Over the years, I've learned to be prepared for the Lord's "out of the blue" leading, so I carry a little extra "God money" with me for situations just like this. I had walked a few steps away, so I turned around and said, "Looks to me like you guys slept in your car."

They could have said, "Wow, aren't you observant?" But they nodded and said simply, "Yes, we did." They were trying to maintain a certain amount of dignity. One of them explained, "We didn't have the money to stay in the hotel, but we're going inside in a little bit. There's an event there that we're going to attend. It's teaching young people about godly leadership."

Now I was sure I was listening to God! I introduced myself and gave them $100. They were very grateful. The money probably paid for their lunches and was enough for the gas to get them home. For me, it was a great pleasure to help them. These two young men were following God with all their hearts and trusting Him to equip them for effective service. God gave me the privilege of being part of their journey. Again, I was a little slow, but it all worked out in the end.

"YOUR WAY OR MY WAY"

Money is a regular component in God Nudges. I remember one of the first services I attended after I became a Christian. I had just received my IRS refund check in the mail. When I went to the service that evening, I had $276 in my wallet. I took out $20 to have hamburgers with my friends after church, and I was going to save the rest. I put the $256 in a secret compartment in my wallet.

When the point in the service arrived for the offering to be taken, I sensed God whisper, "Give the $256 and keep the $20." That was a lot of money for a 19-year-old kid to give away, but I reached into my wallet and took out the money. My gift that day was the beginning of God's financial blessings in my life.

That Fall I applied to enroll in Bible College and I had very little money for tuition, books, and other expenses. I started the semester by paying one-third down, but I had to trust the Lord for the other two-thirds to be paid over the rest of the year. In my first semester, a missionary came to a chapel service. I felt a God Nudge while he was speaking: "Make a $50 monthly commitment to the missions department." This time, the prompting came with a promise: "By the end of the year, you will have given $600 to missions." I didn't see how I could give $600 when I didn't even have the first $50 to spare. I began to argue with God and tell Him there was no way I could give the money.

After I'd made my case to God, He impressed me clearly: "Do you want to do your finances your way or My way?" After a little more conversation with the Lord, I decided to do it His way, even though I still owed two-thirds of my school bill and had no idea where I'd find the money.

Often obedience is the pathway to an outpouring of God's work in us.

When they took the pledges that night, I wrote down on the commitment card that I would support the missionary $50 a month. It was purely an act of faith. God was going to have to supply the money for missions, as well as provide for my school bill—but God's nudge was unmistakable. I was sure I'd heard from Him, so I was confident He would provide.

During the school year, I was able to give my $50 a month pledge. As I look back, I can't tell you how God provided the money for school, but He always came through. Because I was faithful with the pledge, my school bill was paid by the end of the year! I consider it a miracle. Often, obedience is the pathway to an outpouring of God's work in and through us.

The next year, when I enrolled in Bible College, I increased my mission's pledge. That year, someone paid my entire school bill! After attending the college for four years, I left without a dime in school loans—my bills were paid in full—because God miraculously took care of my expenses every semester and every year.

The most important point in this series of events was when God asked, "Do you want to do your finances your way or My way?" I'm so glad I learned the lessons of giving and blessing early in my life.

The Unexpected

Around five years after the night I received a God Nudge and put the $256 in the offering, Karen and I were sitting in a service in Arkansas listening to Rev. Jesse Duplantis. At the conclusion of the service, he gave a word to the congregation. He had received a God Nudge. He said, "When someone here gets home, he's going to receive a check from the IRS."

I thought to myself, Yeah, I bet. The IRS is good about taking money but not too good about giving money. I didn't give it much thought, and Karen and I returned home to Arlington, Texas.

When we went to the mailbox, we found a check from the IRS! It said that we had made an overpayment. My mind instantly raced back to what Rev. Duplantis had said. I thanked God and told Him, "I'll never doubt a God Nudge again!" God blessed us with some extra cash—and for a newly married couple, it was a huge blessing!

Years later when Karen and I planted the church in Oceanside, California, we had nine people and zero money. I believe God has a unique way to plant churches: You start with nothing, and when you get something, you realize it was God who gave it to you.

Jesus had the same situation in His evangelistic association. From reading the Gospels, it seems they were always running in the red. One day, the government came to collect taxes, but the Jesus Evangelistic Association was broke. Jesus gave Peter a God Nudge: "Peter, if you will go down to the lake and pull out a fish, there will be enough money in the fish's mouth to pay your taxes and mine." What an amazing word. If I were Peter, it would have taken a lot of faith to go down to the lake and look for coins in a fish's mouth. But it happened just like Jesus said:

> "Go to the lake and throw out your line. Take the first fish you catch; open its mouth and you will find a four-drachma coin. Take it and give it to them for my tax and yours." (Matthew 17:27)

Sometimes God provides in amazing ways.

SEED MONEY

At one point, Karen and I had enjoyed being in Oceanside for a couple of years. The church had grown, people had gotten saved, and God blessed us tremendously. We grew too big for our temporary site, so we needed to purchase some property to build a facility. Oceanside, California has some of the highest property values in all of America. We had been renting a section of a new shopping center, and the owner told me, "You have an option to buy this property. If you don't buy it, we're going to sell it to a Muslim who's interested in it. He'll be your new landlord."

We had just finished retrofitting the portion of the property we were using, and we didn't have the money to buy the entire shopping center. The price was in the millions of dollars. I had no idea what to do. I'd been seeking God's will, and I'd asked the church to pray as well. We all felt like God wanted us to have the shopping center and use the entire facility for our church, but the money to buy it simply wasn't there.

The shopping center was only four miles from the beautiful Pacific Ocean and located near the center of town. It was a beautiful piece of property—perfect for the church! And it had plenty of parking. After talking with the owner, we were given an extension. He said that if we could come up with a down payment of $240 thousand, he'd finance the rest for us.

It was an amazing offer, but he might as well have said $240 billion! Unless God intervened, we could never find $240 thousand. Karen and I—and the rest of the congregation—continued to ask God to provide.

A week or so later, I left Oceanside to go to Bakersfield, California to attend a District Council meeting. I was asked to receive the offering for the event. As I sat in the service, I thought about what I would say when I took the offering. I thought about the miracle we needed in our own church. I'd been fasting for some time, earnestly praying that God would provide a miracle so that we could purchase the property for the church.

As my mind switched back and forth thinking about the needs of the event and our own needs, I received a God Nudge. The Lord asked me, "How much are you going to give in the offering tonight?"

I was embarrassed. I hadn't planned on giving any money at all. I replied, "Lord, I don't have any money. We paid the bills at the church, and only about $500 is left in our account."

The Lord asked, "How much money do you need?"

I responded, "I need $240 thousand to buy the property."

He said, "You can do one of two things. You can eat your seed, or you can sow your seed. It's your choice."

I knew beyond a shadow of a doubt that the Lord was speaking to me, and His words cut deep into my heart. When the time came for me to receive the offering, I told the congregation, "The church I pastor is in their greatest hour of need. We have about a week left to close on some property we want to buy, but we don't have the money. If we don't come up with $240 thousand, we're going to lose the property we've dreamed of using for our church." I swallowed hard and then continued, "But tonight, the Lord is teaching me that when I have a need, I need to plant a seed. So that's what I'm doing. Tonight, we're giving the last $500 our church has left in the bank."

After praying for the offering, God began to speak to others in the room. "If you've got a need, plant a seed" began to resonate throughout the crowd, and the offering became the largest in the history of the denomination. I was stoked!

However, as I began the long drive home, I began to feel giver's remorse. I thought, what in the world did I just do? I gave all of our money away, and I'm facing the biggest financial crisis of my life!

If you've got a need, plant a seed.

A couple of weeks later, the time was up, but we still didn't have the money. We asked for an extension, and the landowner granted us more time. We kept praying, hoping, and looking for a miracle. One day, I got a phone call. The caller told me, "I heard you speak at the District Council meeting in Bakersfield, and I understand you gave your last $500 as a seed faith offering. A group of us have gotten together and decided to help you. How much money do you need?"

Hope began to rise in my heart. I said, "I need $240 thousand by tomorrow night."

Without a second of hesitation, he said, "Okay, we'll send you the money."

"All of it?" I asked.

"Yes, all of it."

I explained that I didn't have the ability to pay back the money, and our church couldn't qualify for a loan. He explained again, "Pastor, it's a free gift. We're giving you $240 thousand."

That was the day we secured the property for our church in Oceanside. We gave the owner the down payment, and he financed the rest. He gave us such a low interest rate that we were able to make the monthly payments. When Karen and I left Oceanside, the property was estimated to be worth $7 million, but remember, the down payment was obtained from a $500 seed—all for the glory of God.

One of the most effective uses of our money with regard to the God Nudge has to do with those in the service industry. Think about it: when you are being served at a restaurant, the people serving you are usually working for minimum wage and therefore rely on the generosity of people.

It's tragic to be a follower of Christ and not be a good tipper. What is even worse is when your server hears you talking about God or your church and you tip them less than 15%.

The easiest way you can get into a friendly conversation with a person is to be a regular attendee at the same restaurant and give extravagantly. Karen and I have left gratuities three or four times the amount of our meal because we felt nudged by God to do so. As a result of that generosity, we have seen many come to church with us and many have come to Christ.

I encourage you– next time you approach a dining out experience, whisper a prayer:

> "Lord help me to be seated in the section of the person who has the greatest need today."

You will be amazed how many times God will seat you with the right person and how the Holy spirit will whisper an amount for you to give them. Next time you visit, they will want to get to know you and then get to know the Christ in you.

We need to take a good, long, hard look at how we use money. If we use it to wield power, win approval, provide comfort, or achieve safety—instead of trusting God to provide for us and give with an open hand—we need to repent. Everything we are and everything we have belongs to God. We're stewards of all He has entrusted to us, and He wants us to use every penny for His honor and glory. Learning to respond to God Nudges about our money is one of the most thrilling things in life. Don't miss it! If we give generously, cheerfully, and creatively, He'll bless us in incredible ways.

Think about it...

1. What does our use of money say about our hearts?

2. How have you seen God bless you (and others) for being generous givers?

3. What motivates people to give "generously, cheerfully, and creatively"? Who are some examples of people who give like this?

4. What are some ways generosity stimulates our faith? What are some ways it challenges our faith?

5. As you read this chapter, did you sense a God Nudge about your finances? How are you going to respond?

Chapter 8

The Thrill Of Being Spirit-Filled

You can't talk about the God Nudge without understanding the ministry of the Holy Spirit. God's Spirit works in many different ways. He was part of the creation, He led people as they wrote the Scriptures, He is the agent of new birth, He confirms that we're God's adopted children, He leads us into truth, He changes our hearts, and He gives us spiritual gifts so we can be effective in serving God. Many Christians are painfully uninformed about the crucial role the Holy Spirit plays in their lives. When we trust the Spirit to work in and through us, our lives become more exciting than we can imagine, and our world is changed forever!

When I was growing up, many pastors were afraid to talk much about the Holy Spirit. They seemed to avoid the subject. I was raised in a "Bible belt" community in Texas. When I was young, I couldn't figure out why they called it the "Bible belt." It sounded odd to me. Then one day I finally realized it meant if Mom and Dad couldn't get Jesus in my heart through the Bible, they'd beat the devil out of me with a belt! Ahhh, now it made sense.

The little church we attended was full one Sunday morning. Pastor Woods got up and said he had an important announcement to make. "Church," he began cautiously, "I need to let you know that last night I was at a Full Gospel Businessmen's Fellowship, and I was filled with the Holy Spirit."

A few people in the congregation said, "Amen." But Pastor Woods wasn't finished with his announcement. His next statement shocked the church to its core. "I just need to inform you," he paused a moment before completing the sentence, "that I spoke in a heavenly language."

The church became as silent as a tomb. It was like he'd told us he'd become a Communist or was really an alien from Mars. People were stunned.

At the time, I was just a boy, and I wasn't sure what Pastor Woods was talking about. I was very curious why people in the church had been so surprised by his pronouncement. When we went to evening services that Sunday night, Pastor Woods wasn't there. The deacons had met that afternoon and removed him as our pastor. The head deacon addressed those who had gathered for the service that night: "We don't believe that people should speak in a heavenly language—not in this church anyway. We don't believe that the Holy Spirit needs to pass out gifts to anyone, because those gifts were for the formation of the church. The church is already established, and the Holy Spirit went out with the apostles."

Even though the deacons didn't believe in the gift Pastor Woods experienced, the events of that Sunday planted a seed in me. I wondered, *is there more to the Holy Spirit than this church teaches? Am I missing something?*

I began to read the Bible more closely, and I found lots of teaching about the role and ministry of the Holy Spirit. Luke wrote about a Jewish man called Apollos.

> "Meanwhile, a Jew named Apollos, a native of Alexandria, came to Ephesus. He was a learned man, with a thorough knowledge of the Scriptures. [In other words, he knew what he was talking about]. He had been instructed in the way of the Lord, and he spoke with great fervor and taught about Jesus accurately, though he knew

> only the baptism of John. He began to speak boldly in the synagogue. When Priscilla and Aquila [who were a couple of Paul's disciples] heard him, they invited him to their home and explained to him the way of God more adequately." (Acts 18:24-26)

Luke describes Apollos as "a learned man, he had a thorough knowledge of the scripture," but "he only knew of the baptism of John." John the Baptist baptized people who were looking forward to the Messiah. They came to him because they were repenting of their sins. But John's baptism wasn't complete. Priscilla and Aquila recognized that Apollos hadn't received the baptism of the Holy Spirit. They pulled him aside and explained that he needed more than John's baptism—more than just being baptized in water. They then began to explain to him how to be baptized with the Holy Spirit.

Let me ask you a question. Have you ever been baptized with the Holy Spirit? When the Holy Spirit is living in you, you will have more power, more zeal, more love, more joy, and more energy to accomplish the things God has for you. It's the best feeling you will ever have!

The way I think about it is like this: You've just bought a new car with a powerful V-8 engine under the hood. It's shiny red and souped up to the max! It's a fine machine. There's nothing like a new car—the smell, the feel, the ride . . . and especially the looks you get from people as you cruise down the road. You want to say, "Yeah, that's right. It's mine!"

Your new, shiny, red, V-8 powered car will run for a little while, but sooner or later, it'll run out of gas. At that point, it has all the potential in the world, but it will sit on the side of the road until it has a source of power. Gasoline is the source of energy for a car, and the Holy Spirit is the source of energy for Christians. Without depending on Him, we may look good sitting in the pews at church, and we may be able to talk a good game about Jesus, but our hearts will remain cold and empty. The Spirit of God is the source of love, life, and power beyond our imagination.

With cars, we go to the filling station once in a while, but in our spiritual lives, we depend on the Holy Spirit all day every day. Never stop trusting Him to guide you, give you wisdom, and empower you to fulfill God's purposes. When your spiritual tank is full, you'll be able to do some incredible things for God.

Never stop trusting God to guide you.

Many Christians, even in Spirit-filled churches, have misunderstandings about the Holy Spirit. For this reason, I've formulated seven questions to identify and explain His role.

- *Question #1: Does God want me to be Spirit-filled?*

Before He rose back into heaven, Jesus told His followers:

> "I am going to send you what My Father has promised; but stay in the city until you have been clothed with power from on high." (Luke 24:49)

Jesus was making sure they didn't miss the Spirit when He came at Pentecost. He was saying, "You've got a promise coming. Don't miss it! Stick around. You're about to be filled with heaven's power."

Jesus' encouragement wasn't just for the remaining disciples. It applies to every believer. Decades later, Paul explained to the Galatians:

> "He redeemed us in order that the blessing given

> to Abraham might come to the Gentiles through Christ Jesus, [now pay close attention] so that by faith, we might receive the promise of the Spirit." (Galatians 3:14)

You see, God gave every Christian a promise! How good is God's promise? Think about it. Do you know somebody whose promise to you is rock solid, unshakable, and without question going to be fulfilled? I have some friends like that. If we know people who will come through on their promises, don't you think God is going to keep His promises? Jesus often used the word "promise." He told His disciples, "My Father promised you," and "that you might receive the promise." His promise is sure—you can count on it. We only need to get hungry enough to receive the promise of the Holy Spirit.

- *Question #2: Do I need to be Spirit-filled to go to heaven, or is it optional?*

In the opening chapter of the Book of Acts, we read an account of Jesus appearing to His disciples after His resurrection. He appeared to many different individuals and groups over the course of forty days. Before Jesus ascended to heaven, Luke tells us,

> "On one occasion, while He was eating with [the disciples], He gave them this command: 'Do not leave Jerusalem, but wait for the gift My Father promised, which you have heard Me speak about. For John baptized with water, but in a few days you will be baptized with the Holy Spirit.' " (Acts 1:4-5)

Let me stop here for a moment and give you a brief Greek lesson. The way the language is used here is very interesting. I took Greek while I was in Bible College and found it to be one of the most interesting and expressive languages I've ever studied. I learned that there are different kinds of modes and moods that are used in Greek. There is a subjunctive mood (which is a hypothetical situation), and there is also a possibility mode; but the language used in this passage is far removed from all of that. It is a command mode. This basically means that Jesus was giving a command. It wasn't just a suggestion that they go be filled with the promised Holy Spirit. It was His command!

In his letter to the Ephesians, Paul also gives a command:

> "Be very careful, then, how you live—not as unwise but as wise, making the most of every opportunity, because the days are evil. Therefore, do not be foolish, but understand what the Lord's will is. Do not get drunk on wine, which leads to debauchery (self-defeating habits). Instead, be filled with the Spirit." (Ephesians 5:15-18)

What can we expect when we're filled with the Spirit? Later in this passage, Paul tells us we'll be filled with joy and gratitude in our relationship with God, and He'll transform our relationships with people so that we genuinely love them instead of trying to please them to earn their approval, hide from them to protect ourselves, or dominate them by winning every argument. The Spirit's role in giving us nudges is only part of a Spirit-filled life—an important part, but only a part. Being filled with the Spirit revolutionizes every aspect of our lives!

God's magnificent promises and commands of joyful, empowered, wise spiritual life are fulfilled through the work of the Holy

Spirit. He's not an add-on. He's crucial. Some people ask, "Can I get to heaven without being filled with the Holy Spirit?" The answer is, "Yes, you can, but you will be missing out on a lot along the way!" Why in the world would the owner of a fine, powerful car let it sit on the side of the road instead of filling it with gas? Why would a Christian struggle through life with little joy and ineffective service instead of welcoming the Spirit's love and power? It doesn't make any sense at all.

A stubborn heart is one of the biggest obstacles to a wonderful, Spirit-filled life. A story in the Old Testament describes an event when God used a donkey to speak to a man because he wouldn't listen to God. You must know you're not paying attention when God has to use a donkey to talk to you! Balaam was a prophet, but he was extremely hardheaded. One day God got angry with Balaam for not paying attention to the nudge He was trying to give him. If Balaam had kept on in the direction he was going, he would have been heading to his own destruction. So God sent a donkey to stop him:

The Holy Spirit helps us see what we can't see with our earthly eyes

> "When the donkey saw the angel of the Lord standing in the road with a drawn sword in his hand, she turned off the road into a field." (Numbers 22:23)

The donkey saw the angel, but Balaam didn't. The animal got in the prophet's way, so he began to whip the donkey. This happened two more times. Finally, the donkey sat down in the road and spoke to Balaam! The donkey spoke because God was trying to nudge Balaam, but he wasn't listening. I don't know about you, but if a donkey started talking to me, I think I'd pay attention. (Does anybody think of Shrek at this point? Yeah, me, too.)

The Holy Spirit helps us see what we can't see with our earthly eyes. We live in three dimensions, but God lives in all dimensions. The Apostle Paul explained,

> "So we fix our eyes not on what is seen, but on what is unseen, since what is seen is temporary, but what is unseen is eternal." (2 Corinthians 4:18)

Just outside of our dimension of time and space, incredible things are going on. The Holy Spirit helps us pay attention to what God is doing in the unseen realms. God is trying to nudge you and me all the time about what we don't see. I pray every day that God will give me eyes to see the unseen.

I have to admit that on more than one occasion, I've been a lot like Balaam. God has had to break into my life to interrupt me and prevent me from going in the wrong direction. It's like God was speaking through a donkey (or a good friend) to say, "Hey, Knucklehead! You need to change course right now." I don't know if that's how He talks to you, but that's how He has to talk to me sometimes.

God has also used Karen many times to get His point across to me. Sometimes, the message is about our family or our church. Sometimes, it's about things that aren't earth shaking. For instance, I'm a land lover—not much of an ocean guy. I've had a few bad incidents on the water. I've gotten seasick a couple times. I almost drowned. Yeah, that didn't help me, either. I don't care to ever go in the ocean . . . or even near the ocean. Karen tells me all the time, "You don't know what you're missing."

I regularly shake my head, "Don't you know there are sharks

out there?"

She says, "Yeah, but just put your feet in to get your toes wet." I have an answer for that, too. "No, jellyfish are close to shore. And I heard about electric eels. I might get electrocuted!"

We pastored in Oceanside, near San Diego, for fifteen years, and I don't ever remember getting in the water. My wife went to the beach all the time and felt close to God there. She spent hours there praying to God and worshipping. I can pray at my house.

Years ago on a vacation to Cancun, she talked me into snorkeling. I wasn't too happy as we headed out into the shallow water, but I discovered that there are some sweet things just below the surface! We swam out to a little coral reef, and I couldn't believe what I saw. I saw things I'd never seen before. It was amazing! But I've drawn the line at scuba diving. If there's something deeper in the ocean that I need to see, I'll watch the Discovery Channel.

Back to the question: No, we don't have to be filled with the Holy Spirit to get to heaven, but we'll miss far more than pretty little fish in shallow water. We'll miss out on the greatest adventure in life: being led by the God of the universe to touch the lives of people around us.

- *Question #3: What difference will it make if I'm filled with the Holy Spirit?*

I remember the night I was filled with the Holy Spirit. I walked out on the porch and for the first time in my life I realized I'd never noticed the incredible brightness of the stars before. It seemed as though the things around me were clearer, brighter, and more beautiful—like I was really seeing things! As I walked down the sidewalk, it struck me that I didn't have the desires I'd had when I walked into church only hours earlier. I quit five bad habits that night with one encounter of the Holy Spirit. It wasn't magic. The Spirit of God was now filling my heart so that those things were being overwhelmed and crowded out.

Once you experience the Holy Spirit, your life is never the same. You'll realize He's been there all along, and He was working in your life even when you didn't notice Him. The author of Genesis describes an event in the life of Jacob. He had had a very vivid dream one night. God spoke to him and made a promise to him. When Jacob woke up the next morning, he remarked, "God was in this place, and I did not know it" (Genesis 28:16). Realizing the presence of the Spirit shook Jacob's heart—in a good way. He built a memorial, and he stopped at the memorial every time he traveled near it. He didn't want to forget the time he received a God Nudge and stepped into God's dimension.

So what difference does the Holy Spirit make? Before He rose to heaven, Jesus told His followers,

> "But you will receive power when the Holy Spirit comes on you; and you will be My witnesses in Jerusalem, and in all Judea and Samaria, and to the ends of the earth." (Acts 1:8)

We live in a self-absorbed culture, and we're naturally selfish anyway. When the Holy Spirit transforms us from the inside out, our sense of identity and our desires change. We realize we're no longer our own; we've been bought with a price of Christ's blood. We belong to God—body, soul, and spirit—and we live to please Him above all else. We tap into the greatest power source in the universe so God can use us in His mission to redeem the world—people in our families, our neighborhoods, our cities, our nation, and throughout the globe. That's His purpose, and it becomes ours, too. Paul described this commitment when he met the elders from Ephesus. He explained,

> "And now, compelled by the Spirit, I am going to Jerusalem, not knowing what will happen to me there. I only know that in every city the Holy Spirit warns me that prison and hardships are facing me. However, I consider my life worth nothing to me; my only aim is to finish the race and complete the task the Lord Jesus has given me—the task of testifying to the good news of God's grace."
> (Acts 20:22-24)

The Holy Spirit gives us power to be a better witness for Christ and power to overcome life's obstacles through Christ. Some of the obstacles are the bad habits we acquire when we aren't walking with God. On the night I was filled with the Spirit, one of the five habits I stopped doing was cussing. Some people may ask, "What's wrong with cussing? I do it all the time." Maybe you do, but maybe it's time to stop. I've been to a lot of job interviews, and not once did the boss ask how well I could cuss.

> *When you experience the Holy Spirit, your life is never the same.*

A few years ago, we held a special service. The whole evening was devoted to praying for those who wanted to be filled with the Holy Spirit. A few days before the event, a lady came to me and said, "Pastor Mike, I want to be filled with the Holy Spirit." I had a God Nudge and told her, "You're not ready."

"What?" she asked.

I explained, "When we have our service about the Holy Spirit, we'll pray for you. But you're not ready yet. You're still clinging to something—to a habit God wants you to give up. You're not hungry enough for God. Do you know what He wants you to give up?"

She looked down and moaned, "Pastor, you're right. I need to quit cussing."

I said, "That's a good start."

When you give up something, you're demonstrating to heaven that you want more of God. You're not making a deal with Him. You're expressing your deep desire to be fully His.

What difference does being filled with the Holy Spirit make? It will give you power that will help you quit bad habits, and power to accomplish so much more.

• *Question #4: Who is a candidate to be filled with the Holy Spirit?*

In the church were I grew up, I was taught that the Holy Spirit had left the building. He was around for the apostles, but we've been on our own since the first century. I don't know where they got that idea. It certainly isn't in the Bible, and no Bible scholar I know teaches this falsehood. But that's what I'd been taught. When someone told me I needed to be filled with the power of the Holy Spirit, I told him, "I got Jesus when I was saved. That's enough for me."

He answered, "But there's more to it! You're missing the Holy Spirit."

His line of thinking didn't fit my theology. However, after I became Spirit-filled and started reading the Bible, I found passages that turned my life around. For example, Luke recorded:

> "The promise is for you and your children and for all who are far off—for all whom the Lord our God will call." (Acts 2:28)

That means the work of the Spirit didn't stop with the establishment of the original church!

I'm going to ask you a very probing question, and you need to be honest: At some time in your life, have you had a parent? Either a mom or a dad? Of course you have! You weren't hatched, and you didn't come from another planet! Luke is explaining that if you had a parent, the promise is for you—even "for all who are far off." Even for those who are far out, it's for you!

Every believer in Jesus, every person who has been born again, every one who has trusted in His blood to pay for their sins—no matter the race, background, nationality, or horrible sins in the past—is a candidate to be Spirit-filled. That also means that every believer a year from now, ten years from now, a hundred years from now—if the Lord waits that long—is a candidate to be filled with the Holy Spirit. That verse says it's for all who are far off: as far as you can see, as distant as anyone can be, everyone is a candidate to be filled with the same power as the first disciples in the book of Acts.

- *Question #5: Did I not receive the promised Holy Spirit when I was saved or born again?*

John the Baptist said,

> "I baptize you with water for repentance. But after me will come one who is more powerful than I, whose sandals I am not fit to carry. He will baptize you with the Holy Spirit and with fire." (Matthew 3:11)

There were two baptisms: one with water and one with the Holy Spirit and fire. Why fire? Because sometimes there are things in our lives that need to be burned off. The Old Testament prophet, Malachi, explained that God takes us through the fire so that bad habits can just be burned away.

When we become Christians, the Spirit of God comes to dwell in our hearts. For many Christians, the Holy Spirit is a resident, but we haven't made Him our president. When Paul wrote to the Ephesians to tell them to be filled with the Spirit, he was writing to Christians, but many of them weren't Spirit-filled. Daily, deep dependence on God gives the Spirit permission to do anything He wants.

• *Question #6: What must I do to become Spirit-filled?*

The opening chapters of Acts tell us a lot about the role and work of the Spirit. After the 120 in the upper room were filled with the Spirit, Peter preached and 3000 people trusted in Christ. He told them,

> "Repent and be baptized, every one of you, in the name of Jesus Christ for the forgiveness of your sins. And you will receive the gift of the Holy Spirit." (Acts 2:38)

Isn't that good news? The gift of the Spirit is God's promise. All I have to do to be filled with the Holy Spirit is repent of my sins, accept Jesus in my life, and a whole new world of power is given to me. What is that power like? Paul explained that the power available to each Christian is –

> "...the same as the mighty strength He exerted when He raised Christ from the dead and seated Him at His right hand in the heavenly realms, far

> above all rule and authority, power and dominion, and every name that is invoked, not only in the present age but also in the one to come."
> (Ephesians 1:19-21)

We don't get a second-rate power. We receive the same power God used to raise Jesus from the dead! Incredible.

Peter's instruction to the new believers on the day of Pentecost was to repent and be baptized. Some people don't understand why I talk about water baptism in every service at our church. We baptize an average of twenty-five to thirty people a month. Why? Because Peter said, "Repent and be baptized." And why did Peter say that? Because Jesus told us to be baptized. It's your first act of obedience. It tells the world and everyone you know that you're not in charge anymore; you're going to follow Jesus with all your heart.

But what if you don't get baptized in water? Does it really matter? Let me tell you a story. I was at a crusade one day when God was using evangelist Colonel Johann Schonken to perform many miracles. He was praying for a lady, but he stopped awhile and said, "Madam, God is not going to heal you tonight." He paused and then asked, "Have you ever been baptized in water?"

She answered, "No."

He said, "Be baptized in water, and then God will heal your body."

Baptism in water opens up a whole new dimension to you because it's an act of obedience. Any act of obedience we follow from the Bible brings a great reward.

- *Question #7: How long must I wait to receive the filling of the Holy Spirit?*

The Bible talks about a couple of ways people were filled with the Holy Spirit. The first description of the filling of the Spirit was a sovereign act of God. Luke tells us,

> "Suddenly, all of them were filled with the Holy Spirit." (Acts 2:1,4)

Can you imagine! One hundred twenty people were all standing in one place, all there for one purpose, all praising the Lord—and the Spirit of God moved through that place and all of them were filled with the Holy Spirit.

Similarly, Paul experienced the filling of the Spirit in an instant. Luke records the event:

> "Paul was healed and filled with the Holy Spirit, immediately." (Acts 9:17)

How long did he have to wait? It was immediate! And it can immediately happen in your life, too.

NEXT STEPS

By now, I hope you're ready to receive the promise of the Holy Spirit. Let me share three pieces of advice:

1. Come to the Lord with the expectation of being filled.

Have you ever been driving by a row of restaurants and your stomach starts to growl? You smell the smoke of the best barbequed ribs you've ever tasted, and you can't wait to dig in! The closer you get to the restaurant, the smell penetrates your senses, and your mouth starts to water. As you pull into the parking lot, you can't seem to get out of the car quickly enough. You've anticipated the delicious taste of those ribs. Your hunger heightened your expectations.

Sometimes I can look at a crowd of people and see that some people are hungry for more of God. To be honest, there are some people who come to church, who could care less about what God offers them. They're thinking about something else. But a few can't wait to see what God has for them. They expect God to do something special in their lives right here, right now.

We need that kind of anticipation when we ask the Spirit to fill us.

2. Get over the fact that you'll never be holy enough.

The devil tries to convince us that we're not good enough, not smart enough, and not worthy of being filled with the Spirit. He's right. We're not, but we don't plead with God on the basis of our righteousness. We have an Advocate before the Father who pleads for us: Jesus Christ the Righteous (1 John 2:1-2).

No one is holy enough. Not Billy Graham, not Mother Teresa, not you and not me. I've been a Christian for decades and preaching most of those years, and I still can't get holy enough. When we become Christians, our "old nature" is still there, and in fact, it's getting worse every day (Ephesians 4:22)! Every moment of every day, we trust the Spirit to give us wisdom and strength to make better choices as we "put off" selfish, destructive, prideful habits and "put on" compassion, love, joy, and power. But on this side of heaven, we'll never completely become

You will never be holy enough, but you can be hungry enough.

free from sin's presence. As Christians, we've already been delivered from the penalty of sin, we're being delivered from the power of sin, and someday we'll be delivered from the presence of sin. Count on it! Dealing with sin in our lives is like bad Tupperware: You get the lid sealed down on one side, and it pops up on the other side. You get one habit under control, and another one pops up on the other side, and you think. "What happened? I thought I had that under control!"

You'll never be holy enough, but you can be hungry enough. Be honest with God about your sins and failures. Tell Him every day: "Lord, cleanse me, and wash me with your blood. Lord, I know I've got evil thoughts. I know I say stupid things all the time, but Lord, I'm hungry for more of You." I've never seen the hungry turned away from God. Jesus told us, "Those who hunger and thirst after righteousness, they shall be filled" (Matthew 5:6). Those who hunger for God will find Him delightful. Get hungry and stay hungry.

3. If you're asking God to do something He's never done before, He's going to ask you to do something you've never done before.

At our church, I've handed out little sticky red dots. I've asked people to put them on their rearview mirror, their computer monitor, their phone, and any other place so they'll see it every day. I told them that every time they look at the red dot, they're to say these words, "Lord, forgive me of my sins. Cover me with Your blood, and fill me with your Spirit."

Note the sequence:

1) Forgive my sin. That the only prerequisite for being filled with the Holy Spirit.

2) Cover me with Your blood. This is most important because as soon as I ask forgiveness, the Bible says I am forgiven. However, the devil, the accuser of the brethren, comes and magnifies that sin to where all I can think about is that sin. He's a master at getting us consumed with our sins so that we forfeit our candidacy for being spirit-filled. God casts our sin into the sea of forgetfulness. I pray that He covers my mind with His blood so the accuser won't be able to dredge those sins back up and immobilize my experience of being baptized in the Holy Spirit.

3) Fill me with Your Spirit. The Bible tells us: You do not have, because you do not ask God (James 4:2). The Bible also says that:

> "Which of you fathers, if your son asks for a fish,
> will give him a snake instead...how much more
> will your Father in heaven give the Holy Spirit
> to those who ask Him!" (Luke 11:11, 13b)

4) Thanksgiving and praise. Now just finish your prayer with a time of thanksgiving and praise. Thank God He is filling you with the Holy Spirit and praise Jesus with all your heart, soul, mind and body.

5) Expectation. Expect that the Holy Spirit is going to fill you. If you'll pray that way, something is going to happen. Get yourself a red dot, and post it as a reminder to pray. As you seek God, don't be surprised if He tells you to do things that are out of your comfort zone. If Jesus was willing to step out of heaven and come to earth and die, we need to be willing to step across the street to show kindness to a neighbor—especially an annoying one.

Sometimes, God directs us to carve out time to seek Him more fully. He may direct you to begin fasting. Maybe you need to miss a meal so you can have more time to pray, "God, I want more of You, so I'm willing to give up this meal." If you want to have more of God, put something aside. Dial down your worldliness, and dial up your spirituality. You'll be amazed at what God will do in your life.

Think about it…

1. What are some signs a person is hungry for God?

2. How can you tell if you're filled with the Holy Spirit?

3. What are some evidences of spiritual power God offers to us?

4. How does the Holy Spirit enable us to produce the fruit of the Spirit?

5. What are some ways in which God uses suffering to purify our motives, strengthen our hearts, and give us compassion for others who are hurting?

6. What can you give up in order to spend more time pursuing God?

Using The God Nudge in Classes and Groups

This book is designed for individual study, small groups, and classes. The best way to absorb and apply these principles is for each person to individually study and answer the questions at the end of each chapter then to discuss them in either a class or a group environment.

Each chapter's questions are designed to promote reflection, application, and discussion. Order enough copies of the book for everyone to have a copy. For couples, encourage both to have their own book so they can record their individual reflections.

A recommended schedule for a small group or class might be:

Week 1	Introduce the material. As a group leader, tell your story of responding to God Nudges, share your hopes for the group, and provide books for each person. Encourage people to read the assigned chapter each week and answer the questions.
Weeks 2–9	Each week, introduce the topic for the week and share a story of how God has used the principles in your life. In small groups, lead people through a discussion of the questions at the end of the chapter. In classes, teach the principles in each chapter, use personal illustrations, and invite discussion.

Personalize Each Lesson

- Don't feel pressured to cover every question in your group discussions. Pick out three or four that had the biggest impact on you, and focus on those, or ask people in the group to share their responses to the questions that meant the most to them that week.

• Make sure you personalize the principles and applications. At least once in each group meeting, add your own story to illustrate a particular point.

• Make the Scriptures come alive. Far too often, we read the Bible like it's a phone book, with little or no emotion. Paint a vivid picture for people. Provide insights about the context of people's encounters with God, and help people in your class or group sense the emotions of specific people in each scene.

Focus on Application

The questions at the end of each chapter and your encouragement to group members to be authentic will help your group take big steps to apply the principles they're learning. Share how you are applying the principles in particular chapters each week, and encourage them to take steps of growth, too.

Three Types of Questions

If you have led groups for a few years, you already understand the importance of using open questions to stimulate discussion. Three types of questions are *limiting, leading*, and *open*. Many of the questions at the end of each day's lesson are open questions.

Limiting questions focus on an obvious answer, such as, "What does Jesus call himself in John 10:11?" These don't stimulate reflection or discussion. If you want to use questions like this, follow them with thought-provoking, open questions.

Leading questions require the listener to guess what the leader has in mind, such as, "Why did Jesus use the metaphor of a shepherd in John 10?" (He was probably alluding to a passage in Ezekiel, but many people don't know that.) The teacher who asks a leading question has a definite answer in mind. Instead of asking this kind of question, you should just teach the point and perhaps ask an open question about the point you have made.

Open questions usually don't have right or wrong answers. They stimulate thinking, and they are far less threatening because the person answering doesn't risk ridicule for being wrong. These questions often begin with "Why do you think . . .?" or "What are some reasons that . . .?" or "How would you have felt in that situation?"

Preparation

As you prepare to teach this material in a group or class, consider these steps:

1. Carefully and thoughtfully read the book. Make notes, highlight key sections, quotes, or stories, and complete the reflection section at the end of each day's chapter. This will familiarize you with the entire scope of the content.

2. As you prepare for each week's class or group, read the corresponding chapter again and make additional notes.

3. Tailor the amount of content to the time allotted. You won't have time to cover all the questions, so pick the ones that are most pertinent.

4. Add your own stories to personalize the message and add impact.

5. Before and during your preparation, ask God to give you wisdom, clarity, and power. Trust Him to use your group to change people's lives.

6. Most people will get far more out of the group if they read the chapter and complete the reflection each week. Order books before the group or class begins or after the first week.

About the Author

What started out with rough beginnings has blossomed into a full time ministry. Some thought he would go the way of the world but Jesus Christ stepped in when he was nineteen. Mike often quips: "I owe everything to the church. It has given me my friends, a great wife and a purpose for taking up space on the planet."

Mike earned his bachelor's degree from Southwestern Assemblies of God University. He went on to earn his Master's of Divinity from Southwestern Baptist Theological Seminary. He pursued his doctoral studies at Fuller Theological Seminary.

The Robertson's were the pastors of Praise Temple, a church in Burleson, Texas when they received a "God Nudge" to go to Southern California. It was in Oceanside that they planted Family Fellowship Church, and were the pastors there for fifteen years.

Mike then became the Vice President of University Advancement at Southwestern Assemblies of God University (SAGU) in Waxahachie, Texas. In 2008, Mike and Karen became the Lead Pastors of Visalia First Assembly in Visalia, CA.

Resources

I Shook Hands with Death

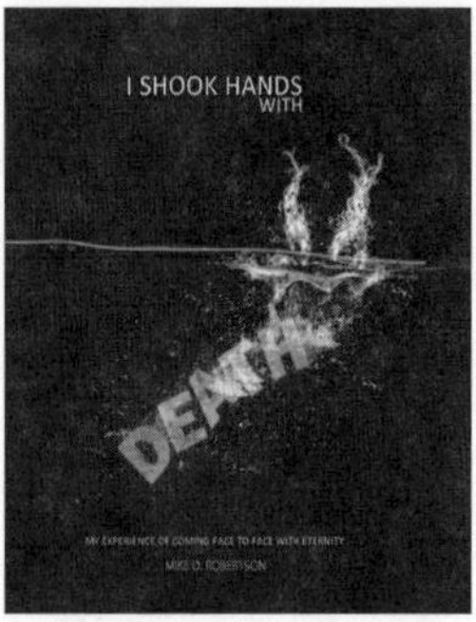

What happens when we die? This question has haunted people since time began. Mike Robertson's near-death experience enabled him to find a clear, comforting answer. When he faced death, he became convinced that he no longer had anything to fear. He had put his life in Jesus' hands, and Jesus would welcome him home.

I Be Jokin'...

The number one problem with public speakers today is that the attention span of the audience has been shortened. Today's culture has been so inundated with sticoms and nine-minute content segments that after about ten minutes, you have lost them.

I think that every 30-minute speech ought to have at least half a dozen points that will make people laugh. Humor endears the audience to the speaker and receptive to what the speaker is saying.

For more information about these and other resources, go to:

www.mikedrobertson.com

Follow Mike on Twitter: @pastormikerob